GREEN
GREEN
GREEN

NIGHTBOAT BOOKS
NEW YORK

GILLIAN

OSBORNE

GREEN
GREEN
GREEN

ISBN: 978-1-643620-32-9

Cover Art: Orra White Hitchcock, "Classroom Drawing of Contortions in Clay Beds, Deerfield, Massachusetts," 1828-1840. Archives & Special Collections at Amherst College (top image). "Olive trees, Mentone, Riviera," between ca. 1890 and ca. 1900. Library of Congress (bottom image).

Design & Typesetting by adam b. bohannon

Text set in Adobe Garamond

Cataloging-in-publication data is available from the Library of Congress

Nightboat Books

New York

www.nightboat.org

CONTENTS

OF THE ECCHO IN GREEN

In his *Theory of Colours*, of green, Goethe writes: "The beholder has neither the wish nor the power to imagine a state beyond it."

A hundred and fifty years later, of "the true Woman, the Mother," Lukács, describing the difference between a monument and a gesture, writes: her longing stops at Earth.

Goethe: there is a placid acceptance in green. Lukács: that we extend to the feminine.

"Hence, for rooms to live in constantly, the green color is most generally selected," one or the other continues. Hence, from Japan, riding my bike between train stations and the school where I worked, I imagined a green kitchen with peonies in California where I might be still. Hence, within that pale green kitchen, I nurtured starters, peeled, chopped, turned, sheltered from the Technicolor.

In Japan, a novice and a Granny Smith Apple are blue. In California, the plum trees bloomed around the same time. My kitchen window looked into a nutritive evergreen that might have been Vermont, which I remembered, except that the outlines were all otherwise: little live oak.

Hence, within another adopted landscape, I crimped a pie, became a mother, grew older. I learned gradually, within that context, a peony would be an impossible, thirsty, pink.

In English, geography is grafted into the etymology of green. The word comes from German (grün), and in nearly all Germanic languages, it carries similar connotations, green as the antithesis to deep winter: fresh, youthful, of grass, of ground, of fruit and vegetables, hopeful, healthy, though also, in this newness, untried or untreated. In England, many places were named for their greenery. Hence, above all, Greenwich. A wich being a settlement, one especially characterized by industry. And Thickly Settled, as signs say along New England by-roads. In upstate New York, everyone pronounced the w: Green-*witch*. Green, in that corner of the country, also being so especially bewitching as to seem almost wild alongside all that settlement. Within weeks, it overruns everything in Massachusetts after epochs of death.

There is also a deathliness built into the linguistic history of green. As in, you look green. As in, lay down. These meanings come from Latin (verdigris) through Greek (chloros), in which green signifies a paleness pertaining to complexion, an excess of bile. Just as the other side of an olive leaf is silver. And drought-resistant plants, in white sun, turn yellowish or gray. So, California, in a drought year, can go blindingly white, not just in the sky, but on Earth, also. And yet, from the Greek word for green, we also have chlorophyll, that transforming substance that mutates nourishment from light. That is green and makes more green, vegetating.

This layering of possible meanings within green is uncanny; what is familiar is already strange. In German, the word for the uncanny comes from a negation of the word for the homely, unheimlich from heimlich, a quick slip, on a prefix's turn, from the cozy to the claustrophobic. So, the Unheimlichkeit of greenery arises from an intuition, built into the very evolution of these words, that there's something sick in the insularity of over-stuffed couches and inward-facing family units.

Something suffocating in the siphoning off of the private from the public green.

All this makes green a tonic color, both harrowing and nourishing. Blue: unadulterated yearning for the infinite. A sky. And yellow: what gets worshipped on Earth, sun and wealth. Green is other to these elementary desires. The idea in green is of the necessity of being with.

We see these meanings of green in William Blake's *Songs of Innocence and of Experience*, where green is the "other" color. The colors being not really colors at all: white and black; silver and gold. Against these binaries, we might call it the middle color: color of melding, mixing; of democracy and striving; of the instability of life as it is actually lived.

"The Ecchoing Green" is also the third poem in Blake's book. The first poem introduces poetry. A speaker cuts a "rural pipe" from a reed and pipes a cheerful song. The second poem introduces the pastoral. A shepherd guards his innocent sheep. There are no colors in these poems. There is music and there is relation: between the poet and his childish audience, between the shepherd and his animals.

"The Ecchoing Green" breaks with the immediacy of lyric expression—a poet, singing—and the generic history of the pastoral—shepherds singing to their sheep from the classical era to Blake's late eighteenth-century—by extending these aesthetic relations into the unsteady dynamism of the social sphere. The ecchoing green is the village green, domesticated green. The poet pipes his songs, like Orpheus, directly into "valleys wild." The shepherd watches his flock in the "sweet lot" of pasturage. But the communal green is where people mix with one another, young and old, playing and slowly fading, ecchoing. Green, as it echoes on the green, is the color of human community: of history, migration, mingling, haunting. With green, the first real loomings of experience, which shade the remaining poems of Blake's collection, emerge.

This transformation—from the innocuous to the ominous—then plays out across three stanzas, which, in turn, in their tripartite arrangement, reinforce the opening triptych of the first three poems. A poem of poetry. A poem of pastoral. A green poem, ecchoing. Innocence, Experience, some middling condition that is not quite one or the other, is both/and. White, Black; Silver, Gold—Green. Among other things, experience is the failure of humans—because of how age, race, class, gender, and what Blake might call unnatural religion mediate mutual perception—to reconcile in a shared middle.

Each stanza concludes with a refrain:

> *On the Ecchoing Green*

> *On the Ecchoing Green*

> *On the darkening Green.*

In the first, the echo is purely innocent, an affirmation of joy, sunshine, bells, birds of song, and spring and spring: the healthful resounding din of children at play. In the second stanza, the echo is already a paler imprint of an earlier occasion of joy, a memory cut off from its original event. "Old John" and "the old folks" remember when they were that young.

Echoing the first poem of the collection and its celebration of lyric immediacy, the first stanza of this poem hums with the immediacy of play. And, just as the second poem is about the pastoral as a genre that reverberates with history, this second stanza is a reminder of the variable spaces and distances between articulation and any echo. How far a song must travel before it finds something against which to fling itself back.

In the final stanza, the sound of the echoing green is substituted for another sense: the darkening green, from which light, and so color, is sapped. Sight isn't the opposite of sound, though. They're merely non-commensurate. There's a half-step in the movement from echo to dark that is dissonant, but gently so, drawing unlike and like into community with one another: immediacy and memory; pleasure and loss. White, Black; Silver, Gold—Green.

This final stanza of Blake's "The Ecchoing Green," as it is with all middling ways, all third colors, is the most open to interpretation. It might simply be a description of the end of the day: boys and girls, come in from play. But the move from present activity to the abstraction of memory might also continue into the wrestling of present and abstraction that is allegory: in which something is this concrete *this* while also being that abstract *that*. A village green that is also the green of graveyards, or of Elysian Fields.

In this same way, American lawns are uncanny. Rarely used, they extend the loneliness of an interior—no public there—into a sterile green a neighbor could evaluate without ever needing to enter. At its inception in America, however, the front lawn was a democratic technology, an extension of the village green to the front door. For centuries, green or empty spaces in Europe were placed at the back of houses, concealing practical household chores or leisure from public view. There, at the back, the lawn later became a feature of British landscape gardening, where it served as a framing device for ornament, or as the designated location for certain kinds of activity—lounging, picnicking, lawn games. The lawn was a private public green. Therefore, unhomely. Familiar but forced.

For a brief period in the nineteenth century, before becoming a symbol of private property in the twentieth—enclosure evacuated of collective activity by the proverbial white picket fence—the American lawn was a space of the commons, a symbol of shared resources, green gone proverbial itself, linking citizen to neighbor. But the American lawn is and has always also been a landscape of erasure, as we see in Whitman's conundrum, in "Song of Myself," over the significance of grass.

Whitman is not, like Blake, a poet of innocence and experience. He prefers experience, which has the privilege of ecstasy. When he lets a child into "Song of Myself," however, the child asks, "What is the grass?" What is green? It is a simple question, though like other innocent questions, impossible to answer. It could be anything, Whitman's lyric speaker offers. Hieroglyph, handkerchief of god, the hair of rotting corpses, a democratic pact. "Growing among black folk as among white." Black, White; Silver, Gold—Green.

Because grass can grow almost anywhere—like the faux-Scottish Highlands of golf courses in Dubai or Palm Springs—lawns invoke an elsewhere. A village green that sometimes exists in New England and certainly exists in Celebration, Florida, but has largely ceased to be used as in Blake's "The Ecchoing Green." Or which has maintained only the absence of allegory: an ethereal pasture made of more imagination than material. Grass overwrites the particular characteristics of bioregions, mowing geography over, subsuming distinctions into ubiquitous turf.

The lawn absorbs multiplicities within a single figure, subsuming species of grass into a singular vegetable entity, presenting a gathering of individuals as a unified field. Kentucky bluegrass, crabgrass and other species common to the American lawn—few of them native to the Americas—become one, melting pot combining with salad bowl into a green averse to history. History means sharing a past, present, future world. History at its best is green as Mt. Auburn Cemetery—which was designed before, and so includes, the Civil War—is green. A place for the dead, designed for collaborative strolling among the dead and the living. One should be allowed to picnic there right now.

It's only since the 1970s that green, in German and English, has signaled the Earth. When that word was adopted, for environmental advocacy, there was an inexplicit acknowledgment of the two seemingly conflicting etymologies of green: the fresh and the fetid; springtime and sickness. And an acknowledgment of allegory: that a color could stand for a condition of verdure, ailing, on a planetary scale.

Allegory implies that something more real is taking place outside a text. The proper nouns that pin together the tapestry are also rents in its fabric. Love has a life in language, and in the garden down the hall and through the door.

An external perspective runs through the allegory of Blake's poem, further opening it to contexts beyond those any book might contain. In the penultimate line of each stanza, the one before the refrain, Blake injects a passive construction that insinuates an unseen seer into each scene:

> *While our sports shall be seen*
> *On the Ecchoing Green.*

> *In our youth time were seen*
> *On the Ecchoing Green.*

> *And sport no more seen*
> *On the darkening Green.*

The verb tenses slide from subjunctive, to past imperfect, to simple past, but the passivity of each remains consistent. This lurking, unnamed, looker is the first imposition of a god in *Songs of Innocence and of Experience*, and it should be spooky because it is also that middle way, that living green that echoes and darkens, an outside that is in everything, haunted humankind. Silver, Gold; Black, White—Green.

Turning from the human, though not fully, the final stanza of "The Ecchoing Green" also unfixes time from narrative linearity in its first line: "Till the little ones weary." Is this "till" retrospective or prospective? Have the actions of the final stanza already happened? Or are we stranded, in the space between stanzas, until some yet to be disclosed requirement is met?

Of the "Allegorical, Symbolical, Mystical" uses of green, Goethe writes: "In this there is more of accident and caprice" and "the meaning of the sign must be first communicated to us before we know what it is to signify; what idea, for instance, is attached to the green color, which has been appropriated to hope?"

Green is an echoing color, a space of meeting and reverberation at the middle of the spectrum. So if this is a book about a color, about when and how a color becomes material, there are many greens in it—a repetition of green that is also an articulation of difference each time it is voiced—a catalogue of green in which things are stripped of the fullness of context and yet vibrationally, referentially, living—the seasonal disorders of green across arguing geographies—the California winter, cloaked in wet—and the riot of midsummer along the eastern western rolling hills of New York—the entanglement of biography and biology—the sacrament of shared lives and dependencies—the fitting together of fungi and algae into lichen—the ribbing of blood in veins, sap in leaves—green green green, without punctuation, paratactic and aligned.

READING NATURAL HISTORY IN THE WINTER

For years, I've been trying to write an essay about reading natural history in the winter. That essay began one spring or early summer in upstate New York when it became apparent to me that a simple list could invoke emotions—expectations, sorrows—with no direct correlation to any of the things named or described.

The essay began before writing began—more on that in a minute. But when I did finally begin writing, I was in the early years of graduate school in California, and the most recent multi-year drought had yet to prevent farmers from planting their fields in the middle of the state. It was winter, then, in California, and the hill we lived on was so green it was difficult to imagine it becoming its summer color again: tawdry gold, spicy with feral radish.

Now, where I am writing, it is towards the end of another unseasonably warm October in Massachusetts. Or now, where I am rewriting in Massachusetts, it is snowing in April. And again, returning to this still unsettled series of reflections, mid-June, many years later, on the verge of moving back to California, everything on the East Coast, a riot of green. And finally, in California again, another wet, green winter, the sound of it rushing over rocks toward the Pacific.

California had given me a different kind of seasonal disorder from the dull winter headaches I'd grown up with. Those required artificial light boxes. These produced irises in winter. And that disjuncture—this fullness inside a time I felt should be barren—taught me something about seasons. How, stitched to the running onward of historical time, there is something disruptive, disordering, in their manifestations, so that, though spring is entirely expected, still, it startles and delights, and nothing can prepare us for New England's blank chill. California's failure to graft effectively onto the seasons I'd known, that were harsher than seasons in England but still recognizable across the Atlantic, alerted me for the first time to seasons within seasons.

Wallace Stevens, who never crossed the Atlantic, said there was a season after winter and before spring. But English doesn't often go there. Other languages do a better job of getting at seasons in-between. In Japanese, there are traditionally twenty-four seasons, the year unfolding along a series of small recursions. Spring begins when winds melt ice, turns around the equinox with distant thunder, and peaks with peonies. German has a nachsommer, a summer after summer. In New England, this is Indian Summer, as if that stolen season could only be accounted for by a covert confession of cultural displacement. In French, there's a spring before spring: avant-printemps, which Francis Ponge documented from a house in the countryside in the early 1950s in a book which wasn't published until the Paris political "Spring" of 1968. There's a belatedness and a prescience in the in-betweenness of seasons that wrests us from history, directing attention toward possible worlds: "then" or "then." And seasons are also that past or future eventfulness that rattles us in the guise of an ice storm, here and now. This essay is about how writing takes place within scenes of experience, and in the presence of other writing, which, through the friction of living on language, produces that seasonal jolt: the unsettling impulse of then within now.

Reading first: within that earlier California winter, I was reading about gardening in antebellum New England. I wasn't a very responsible reader back then, even if a very responsive one. I didn't know yet why I was reading so much about gardens. Now I can say with assurance: I was excavating texts for the seasons of my childhood. California was full of plants colonized from around the globe: fresh and frilly with eucalyptus and bottlebrush from Australia, spiky with South American ice plants along the coast. But I missed the flowers I'd known the names of as a child the way I missed old friends: crocus, lilac, peony.

Looking for New England, though, I found California in my reading. I'd happened upon a list published in *The Horticultural Register and Gardener's Magazine* of flowers blooming and fading in a garden in Boston on "the 29th of October, 1835." That list began with a California poppy, a perennial rarely if ever seen in eastern gardens today, and grown as an annual when it is, and ended with another plant, the bright, droopy, blue star of lobelia. After each scientific name, the authors noted the stage at which they discovered each species that October day, which was itself a warm one, though more "favorabl[y]" so: individuals were "in perfection," "going off," "just opened," "bearing seed," "some lingering stragglers still pretty," "very gay," "hardly yet in perfection," and so on.

> Eschscholtzia Californica, in perfection.
> Convolvulus major and minor, the last in perfection.
> China asters, many varieties, going off.
> Chrysanthemum tricolor and indica, several varieties, just
>   opened.
> Indian pinks, great varieties, in perfection.
> Dahlias, several varieties in perfection, including several
>   seedlings from seed sown in the open ground in May.

Marvel of Peru, six varieties, in perfection.

Balsams, going off.

Salvia splendens, in great beauty bearing seed.

S. Prismatica, in perfection.

S. Angustifolia, in perfection.

Canna indica, red and yellow, second shew of bloom in perfection.

Commelina caelestis, in perfection.

Talinum ciliatum, in perfection every sunny day.

Anagallis indica, a few of its beautiful blue flowers.

Dracocephalum speciosum, going off.

Marygold, varieties, in perfection.

Petunia nyctaginiflora, in perfection.

Golden rods, going off.

Sevia Serrata, in perfection.

Reseda odorata, mignonette in great perfection.

Sweet peas, some lingering stragglers still pretty.

Gladiolus natalensis, in beauty.

Violas, heartsease in profusion, very gay.

Iberis odorata in perfection.

Stock gilliflower, rose colored, very spicy odor, in perfection, new.

Verbena aubletia, in perfection.

Ximenesia enceloides, going off.

Coreopsis lanceolata, the last flowers, elegant, yet in beauty.

Jacobea, several colors, hardly yet in perfection.

Galinsogea tribolata, in perfection. We have given this a bad character in our article in the preceding number, it is just to say that it increases in beauty as the autumn advances.

Nicotiana repanda, in perfection.

Browallia elata, blue and white, in perfection.

Silene, several varieties, going off.

Orobus niger, going off.

Calceolaria pinnata, in perfection.

Silver hawkweed, a few flowers.

Picridium tingitanum, a few flowers but perfect.

Hibiscus trionum, a few flowers small.

Centaurea sweet sultan, in beauty, C. Cyanus also.

Delphinium ajacis, the double branching larkspur, in great
     beauty, 4 feet high, one plant with 30 branches of beautiful
     blue flowers.

Madia Splendens, in beauty.

Malope grandiflora and trifida, in perfection.

Zinnia, varieties, going off.

Poppy, picotee, second blooms, small but yet handsome.

Ammobium alatum, a few blooms left.

Zeranthemum annuum, yellow and white, in perfection,
     lucidum going off.

Oenothera, several varieties, particularly tetraptera, in
     perfection.

Coronilla securidaca, in perfection.

Eutoca multiflora, just going off.

Lopezia coronata and racemosa, in great beauty.

Plectocephalus americanus, great American Thistle, in perfection.

Gilia Capitata, in perfection.

Lobelia gracilis, in perfection.

Some of these, I still don't know how to picture. Many no longer adhere to these particular names. Some were as common as hostas, from Asia, on front lawns where I am from. Some, like California poppies, have become less common. But my discovery of the list then was not about an encounter with particularity, or even history, but of accumulation. Yes, I could have said to Kierkegaard, a repetition is possible. A sequence is a moving thing.

At that time, I could still identify with Emily Dickinson's definition of poetry: that you know what it is when you feel the top of your skull flying off and you get so chilly from that wound that no tropic breeze could ever thaw you. For me, that feeling was more of being dropped from a great height so that the Earth, when I arrived there, was greedy for lungs.

That list, stuttering around perfection, of a half-dead garden on the other side of the country more than a century ago on the edge of a new season, gave me that feeling. Which made me realize: how barren and barely a thing was a poem.

In his essay "The Poet," written in the vicinity of Boston a decade after the compilation of this list, Ralph Waldo Emerson describes how "bare lists of words are found suggestive, to an imaginative and excited mind." A list in a gardening manual can act on a reader like a poem. But this action depends on other surrounding conditions. My responsiveness to this particular list was the result not only of an ongoing seasonal disorder induced and maintained by geographic displacement, but also by an encounter with a previous list.

Its conditions were this: someone I had known all my life and yet never really known, someone my mother had known all her life and yet never really known, was dying. She was a great lover of the natural world, particularly of birds and plants. This was one thing we did know about her.

She would ask my grandfather to stop by the side of the road on family vacations in the West so she could cup a flower in her hands. I wish I had an image of this memory that was never mine. A woman, palming something living along the side of the road. To tell you the name of the flower she was sheltering, I would need to ask her—but she is, as I was saying, no longer alive. Meanwhile, my grandfather would grumble because there was a destination and because he was a philosophy professor. He wrote books about ethics and education, subjects I find, when philosophically treated, too exhausting to keep up with. He wrote me long letters that were lectures disguised as intimations.

There are many books that I would like to read that I have not read, a fact which some days I attribute to laziness or distraction, and other days, to the fact that I am a relatively busy person and am trying to be a decent parent and partner and keep a relatively clean house and attend to the underappreciated edges of things, in addition to getting my reading done. All of this is a way of saying: I have never read my grandfather's books and I doubt I ever will.

But, as you will perhaps have gathered, it was my grandmother, Rosemary, whose list I encountered, which changed my understanding of what poetry was or could be. Generally, I was afraid of her. Not because she was unkind. But because she didn't say things. The things she had to say were disguised in bird feeders and poppies. The last time I saw her she gave me a jar of honey. I still have the jar though the honey is gone.

As a rule, I only appreciated her gifts after the fact. The blue glass bowls she gave me when I was eight and utterly uninterested in kitchens, and that I have been baking with since leaving home. Meaning, she was a precocious giver, a personality flaw I can relate to, now that I have a child to whom I give books that exceed an appropriate reading level. Like William Blake and William Blake. Or *Over and Over* by Charlotte Zolotow, which is a picture book from the 1950s about mostly Christian holidays and the seasons and a little girl who is so little that she "doesn't understand what time is." Though everyone else did, my grandmother rarely gave me books and never gave me this one, but it was one of my mother's favorites. One of my favorites, too. Which means, over and over, reading happened. Reading happened to us.

In *Over and Over*, there is a yellow crocus the little girl remembers, but doesn't remember where or when she saw it last. The ones that came up in our side yard were deep purple with yellow cores. Though this was one of the flowers I missed most, it isn't a New World plant, native neither to the Northeast or California. Memory seems personal, but it accumulates collectively, through centuries. The fact that the history of these common denizens disappears within the human names and dates and atrocities of history means that, like this little girl, very few of us have a handle on what time is, how it snaps continually against geography.

Recently, when rereading this children's book over and over at bedtime, I realized how much the little girl in this picture book is like Isabel in Herman Melville's novel, *Pierre, or the Ambiguities*, a character who also has difficulty with time. Isabel narrates events out of order: men scale trees over an ocean and then they are in the rigging between masts of a ship; bodies are carried out through windows and then they are dead.

When I was first living in California, I became obsessed with her disorders, which she calls "bewilderingness": both her backward narration, and how her story sticks like a bur, the only first-person voicing, in the unfolding plot of *Pierre*, and the fact that she only comes to know herself through the identification of things living and dying around her. I am not a cat she comes to accept. Not a snake, or a lightning bolt. Not a blasted tree. Therefore, I must be human. This deduction of humanness from the non-human surround makes an experiential sense. Whatever I am has to do with that crocus, that chipmunk, that orchard and marsh.

This is different from saying I carry such things or places with me. It's closer to being infused with an inhumanness gifted by these non-human encounters. The dissertation about Isabel I spent years writing and rewriting and erasing eventually had to be abandoned. How many drawers are filled with abandoned books about *Pierre*, my advisor said. Writing about Isabel, I had thought I was writing about this inhuman heart to the human, that makes narration impossible, which might make a claim for poetry, as a different way of telling. Now, I'd say that the vectors of motivating indirection that compelled that reading were also about seasons, and geography, and reading. In Isabel's narrative disorders, I recognized my own seasonal disorder. From a windowless office-garage in California, I stared at Google Earth images of the Berkshires, looking for August with its heat-lightning there.

In *Pierre*, Melville describes the feelings Isabel produces in others, and that she certainly produced in me, as an "ineffable correlativeness": a feeling that this connects to this that can't be fully verified because feeling is inevitably in excess of the facts; the head a gaping hole and a cold wind blowing through. Isabel's story focuses on her childhood. And Pierre describes Isabel as childish, even as he's ineffably attracted to her. These suggestions of incest—Isabel is Pierre's half-sister—contributed to the definitive failure of *Pierre*, and the end of Melville's viable run as an acknowledged author. But the attribution of sexual allure to a child-like waif is rampant in nineteenth-century literature and wouldn't by itself have caused alarm. In fact, the other love-object in *Pierre*, the Romantically-named Lucy, is, like Wordsworth's Lucy, bright and child-like and doomed.

In the nineteenth century, women were childlike by association, in that they made and cared for children and because, in their economic, and often physical, weaknesses, they needed to be cared for, too. Women who wrote, or appeared in poems in the period, almost inevitably position themselves, or are positioned, in relation to this childishness: either as nurturing mother (see Lydia Sigourney), or unavailable and therefore ultimately innocent temptress (see Frances Osgood), or child-bride (this type appears generally in novels and poems by men—see Charles Dickens and Edgar Allan Poe). Women sometimes also wrote from the perspective of children for children, but these poets remain, for the most part, firmly archived in periodicals and albums, interesting only to scholars. Emily Dickinson is one of the only nineteenth-century poets who is still widely read who writes *as* a child, though not *for* children.

In his first encounter with her, Thomas Wentworth Higginson either picks up on, or projects, that child-like quality of nineteenth-century femininity onto this poetess. Reporting their meeting in a letter to his wife, Higginson refers repeatedly to Dickinson's "quaint" and "child-like" demeanor: she enters the room with "pattering footstep like that of a child"; places daylilies in his hand "in a childlike way"; and apologizes, "in childlike fashion, 'Forgive me if I am frightened; I never see strangers, and hardly know what I say.'"

But she does know what she says. In the course of their conversation, she says many memorable things regarding poetry, most memorably, that statement I've already referenced several times: that poetry is ice and headlessness. Dickinson's readings are responsive. The nineteenth-century poet and physician Oliver Wendell Holmes would call them "physiological"; a twentieth-century critic might call them a "psycho-aesthetics"; a twenty-first-century poet: a "(soma)tic ritual." The body, in all its irrational histrionics, gets involved. Poetry is recognizable not by its form, but in its effects. This is fundamentally a childish method of reading. It's the way I read before I was trained to read otherwise. In thinking about reading natural history in the winter, I've been trying to take seriously that earlier, pre-educated, readerly sensibility. Because I think it does get at something crucial: the way surroundings—seasons, geography, the amorphousness of experience—infiltrate books. The narrative experiments of the early twentieth century—stream of consciousness and all that—aimed to show how psychology pervades everything. I'm interested in how everything pervades psychology, mediated by language, especially in its barest forms. A poem, or a list, makes space for the world to enter in ways that narrative excludes.

Dickinson defines reading natural history in the winter in a letter to Higginson in 1877. Masquerading as a child again, she writes: "When Flowers annually died and I was a child, I used to read Dr Hitchcock's Book on the Flowers of North America. This comforted their Absence – assuring me they lived." Dickinson's formulation of reading natural history in the winter hinges on what isn't there, on "Absence." Despite the appearance of a possessive pronoun before its introduction, "their Absence" has multiple possessors: "Flowers," de-activated by winter, or the reader, who feels that empty space of dormancy acutely, and, in compensation, turns to a book. There is also the absence of the childish reader Dickinson once was within the adult writer she has become. That absence—of then within now—is a hallway of mirrors: she remembers reading that was remembering. This circularity makes a reader seasonal, too.

In "My Out-Door Study," an essay first published in *The Atlantic Monthly* in 1861 and reprinted in multiple volumes across the remainder of the nineteenth century, Higginson also refers to the benefit gleaned from reading natural history in the winter: "Even the driest and barest book of Natural History is good and nutritious," he writes, "if it represents genuine acquaintance." Although Higginson was elsewhere a booster for the pursuit of regional science, the potentials he identifies in the reading of natural history fall outside the goal of forwarding nationalist knowledge of American backyards. Whereas the naturalist ventures into the field in search of new discoveries, the "good" that comes of natural history reading derives from preexistent "acquaintance." A reader simply revisits scenes and species she already knows: "one can find summer in January by poring over the Latin catalogues of Massachusetts plants and animals in Hitchcock's Report," Higginson writes. One can find California in Massachusetts while reading natural history in a California winter a century after the fact.

There is also an absent book in Dickinson's letter. The book through which she mediates both "Absence" and assurance—Edward Hitchcock's "Book on the Flowers of North America"—isn't actual: a "barest" book so bare it never existed at all. Hitchcock published a *Report on the Geology, Mineralogy, Botany, and Zoology of Massachusetts* in 1833, an initial survey that led to a more comprehensive survey of the commonwealth, commissioned by the legislature and conducted by a team of naturalists between 1839 and 1846. Or earlier, the year before Dickinson was born, the Junior Class at Amherst, who had followed Hitchcock into the field in search of specimens and listened to his botany lectures, paid for the printing of his *Catalogue of Plants Growing Without Cultivation in the Vicinity of Amherst College* in 1829.

Dickinson may be misremembering, or re-imagining, the scale of either of these studies, expanding Amherst or Massachusetts to the scope of North America, an extension from the local to the general that is not so surprising for a poet who elsewhere called Amherst "Eden." Hitchcock catalogues "Plants"; Dickinson remembers, or imagines, more particularly, "Flowers." And while Hitchcock records his findings in a scientific *Catalogue*, Dickinson remembers a more generic "Book." Read through the absence of a book that doesn't actually exist but stands in relation to parts and wholes—angiosperms and the vegetable kingdom, region and continent, the memories of a child and the life that absorbs them, a catalogue and a book, and seasons within the year—Dickinson's experience of reading natural history in the winter is an example of how context echoes within text, how what is reverberates with what is no longer quite as fully there.

Hitchcock's "Reports," in their variant verisimilitudes, connect to another important mid-nineteenth-century articulation of reading natural history in the winter: Henry David Thoreau's first published essay, a review of the collective endeavor of Hitchcock's *Report* for the July 1842 issue of *The Dial*. Thoreau begins that essay: "Books of natural history make the most cheerful winter reading." And continues: "I read in Audubon with a thrill of delight, when the snow covers the ground, of the magnolia, and the Florida Keys, and their warm sea breezes; of the fence-rail, and the cotton-tree, and the migrations of the rice-bird; of the breaking up of winter in Labrador, and the melting of the snow on the forks of the Missouri; and owe an accession of health to these reminiscences of luxuriant nature." While Dickinson finds things—beloved flowers—in the absence of winter, and Higginson finds one season slotted in another—summer in winter— Thoreau finds geography interrupting time and place—Florida and Canada and the Midwest in Massachusetts. Traveling through Keys and along melting ice-flows, Thoreau improves his health through "reminiscences" of scenes he has never actually seen. For Thoreau, reading natural history in the winter is an act of imagination; for Higginson: memory and recovery.

For Dickinson: both/and.

Reading natural history in the winter recreates the scene of writing, flooding the bareness of transcription with the fullness of every thing living and dying outside books. The book, or the poem, or the list, becomes a window. The window opens onto time and place. Mt. Greylock, which Melville could see from his window while writing *Moby Dick* and *Pierre*, and to which he dedicated that latter novel. Nathaniel Hawthorne, whom Melville likewise considered through the veil of fiction, and to whom he gave his *Whale*. California; Amherst. The fullness of the scene of reading is a window that moves through and mediates time and space, like a "Short Talk" by Anne Carson, "On Reading," that I began reading the year before I discovered the list of flowers, some of them in perfection, in a Boston garden in October 1835; the year after my grandmother died.

Carson's prose-poem begins with the simplest of plots: parents, children, journeying together, divided by what they love and hate. "Some fathers hate to read but love to take the family on trips. Some children hate trips but love to read." What happens next is not narrative. Instead of story, the sheer factualness of context interrupts a well-appraised realism: a young reader sees "the stupendous clear-cut shoulders of the Rockies from between paragraphs of *Madame Bovary*." These merge: mountain and woman, the geologic and the embodied, the present of reading and memories of that present-past. Ever after, that reader does "not look at hair on female flesh without thinking, Deciduous?"

Poetry is so profoundly ineffectual because, among other features, it either lacks narrative (in lyric), or draws attention to itself in ways that go beyond narrative (even in epic or narrative forms). It doesn't go anywhere, and so it goes round and round in space and time. Reading natural history in the winter prioritizes past encounters with materials and present experiences of reading over a utopic future sometimes promised by appeals to narrative as the best or only thing literature has to offer. Literary critics have often loved futures: Arnold heralded it; Ransom welcomed a criticism "before us"; see Jameson on utopia. But history, including its futures, doesn't work the way it used to. Species are dying off as we read. So it's not enough to read into what's coming. What's here, now? In California, this winter, a poet drove to work wearing a gas mask because of the forest fires burning in suburban backyards.

Reading is one of the only technologies flexible enough to respond to what it feels like to read in a world in which the material transformations of time are faltering. Even as climate change revises the seasons—infiltrating their motions with vacancies and pre-maturities—the seasons remain inhuman, anti-narrative, both in and out of time. Their predictability is not the predictability of romance, but of a refrain. Their bells ring not for weddings but for the repeatability of lives and deaths. Spring, spring, spring again.

It's not just spring, though. There is something excessive in all responsiveness to seasons, to lists of natural history, or to poems. That excess arises because the conditions of present environments can be so demanding that they override memory or imagination. So, winter lasts forever. "I now *know*," writes Jamaica Kincaid, reading gardening catalogues in a bathtub in Vermont in early March in the 1990s as I was just across the state border, a teenager reading sonnets in the bathtub in the winter, "that spring will never come." Reading natural history in the winter focuses that excess, as winter, or other seasons, or other climatological effects, infiltrate attention. That divided attention, like so many of the radical writing practices of the twentieth and twenty-first century, is capaciously open to what lives outside of books as well as in them; reading natural history in the winter resists closure, calls out. But lyrically. It encounters the self through the ways a self is situated: irregularly composed.

When I read the "fir flanks" of Carson's Emma's Rockies, I was also rereading Eliot's Prufrock's aversions: "I have known the arms already, known them all, / Arms that are braceleted and white and bare / (But in the lamplight, downed with light brown hair!)." And the half-empty Oakland apartment I lived in my first semester of graduate school, and the springtime in New York years earlier, all the running up and down stairs and the magnolia trees shedding on the way toward indecency and rapture and Eliot's lines flickering through it all.

At a recent professional meeting, a professor of material science—he defined his field to me afterwards as "how to build a habitable planet"—described a hike he had taken with colleagues and friends over a long weekend in the dark. Sitting on top of a mountain before dawn, ragged lines of firs, perhaps, skirting the edge of a rocky opening, or a fire-tower splitting the stars into quadrants and angles, he found himself reflecting on the forgetfulness of his students. If only he could teach them *here*, he thought, deliver a lecture on top of a mountain at night (read a poem in a bus shelter in autumn), how much more might they remember. Something about the context, he thought, seared content, fused it with experience, locked it away in some salvageable memory vault.

I remember *Don Quixote* better than Thucydides, not because it was fiction rather than history, but because I fell asleep while reading by an open window. I remember the fourth book of the *Aeneid* not only because Dido's ravaging grief is terrifying and gorgeous, not only because the neat civilizing boundaries of the city are invaded by deer and other wild beasts, but also because I was rushing up Amsterdam Avenue to meet someone I hadn't seen in a year but thought I was still probably in love with. Animation of even the most elaborate of literary endeavors depends not only on reading, but also on the contexts of reading. Stevens on a suburban golf course at night; Sartre in a seedy park; Said on a beach, surrounded by topless spring-breakers. Reading takes place.

The last time I saw my grandparents together, they were living in a home that was not their home. When they'd packed up that old white farmhouse in western New York, Rosemary had thrown away all the slides of family vacations to the West without consulting anyone. But she'd never documented all those roadside flowers, so what was there to hold onto? Before that, when we were born, she'd planted a tree. I was the ornamental hardwood, peeling and tarnished, outside the window of the room where she slept alone.

Now, she'd asked the gardeners to leave the little hill she could easily see from another window so it could seed itself. She wrote the names of little things she knew by sight:

Dandelions
Daisies
Hawkweed
Moth Mullein
Equisetum
Dianthus
Thistle
Coltsfoot
Queen Anne's Lace
Poppy
Wood Sorrell
Butterfly Milkweed

Pick ?
Heal-all
Evening Lychnis
Curley (?) Dock
Smartweed
Milkweed
St. John's wort
Blue Eyed Grass (?)
Purple Vetch
Red Clover
Birds Foot Trefoil (?)
Daisy's
Black Medic (?)
Honeysuckle
Pussy Willow
Buttercups
Purple Loosestrife
Knapweed
Phragmites
Butterflyweed
Teables ?
For-get-me-not

She actually wrote the final entry like that, full of dashes, like Dickinson had infected this pale blue flower.

There's something sentimental about grandparents, and seasons, flowers, and poetry, which is why nineteenth-century poets, and especially women, wrote about all these topics, and were considered children.

But my grandparents were hard, twentieth-century, Midwestern people who didn't demonstrate much love toward each other and who I couldn't ever bring myself to really love. I spent part of one summer living with them to attend a writing course at the university where my grandfather worked. After writing, I'd spend so long lying on the lacey bedspread of the guest room staring out a window at a gray barn to avoid talking to them that when I finally came downstairs (to go outside to the garden and fields), I had a doily emblazoned on my cheek.

That last time I saw them, I'd recently finished college, and I'd written some things that someone had liked: a long essay on poetry as a performance of illness and dying in Dickinson and Shakespeare and Donne. And poems. This essay is another version of that essay, and maybe I only have one essay ever to write, over and over. I don't remember any of the poems, though I wanted, above all, to be a poet.

My grandfather, the professor, was full of praise about the essay. Dismissive of the poems. What word did he use to dismiss them? It may have been "childish." And then, Rosemary, with her list that was a poem. In the nineteenth-century sentimental language of the flowers, Rosemary stands for remembrance, an evergreen from a warmer place, that won't let go when winter arrives.

Maybe this is an essay about why I never could become a poet or a professor or a gardener. Or about why reading the unliterary is like writing poems. It was summer then, or early spring, when everything still is nearly dead. Why reading and writing poetry is really like nothing at all.

OF THE
VICINITY OF

Of Introductions

When Emily Dickinson met Thomas Wentworth Higginson, she handed him day lilies—as an "introduction."

In another letter, to another minister, Dickinson would write: "A Blossom is perhaps an introduction, to whom – none can infer."

Of Flowers

In the likely winter of 1877, Dickinson to Higginson: "When Flowers annually died and I was a child, I used to read Dr Hitchcock's Book on the Flowers of North America."

In the spring before she was born, the Junior Class at Amherst, who had been attending Edward Hitchcock's lectures on botany, paid for the publication of their professor's *Catalogue of Plants Growing Without Cultivation in the Vicinity of Amherst College.*

Many of these were Flowers, though not All.

Of Amherst

Of the local poem in a global age, Jahan Ramazani writes, the local is "the microcosmic obverse of the global, on which it obliquely depends." He continues, "in poetry, which often has an especially long memory," any particular place may be "mediated through a tissue of radial connections to poems of other times and places."

Of Amherst, for example, see Dickinson, who writes: Eden.

Over a red, red rose, volunteering in a garden at the Emily Dickinson Museum, a facsimile of a fantasy of the original, we read a poem. To help the roots catch firmly into dirt. This was late spring, 2018, and the cultivation of roses began in China 5,000 years ago or so.

Of Windows

I have been reading Emily Dickinson perennially since the summer I was 20, and living in France for the second time, if passing through without belonging can be called living, if it reorders the mind as my initial sad months there did. Previously, I hadn't made it all the way around a year to summer. Rain and rain and rain. That summer, the summer of Emily Dickinson, I wasn't sure I wanted to be living with the man whose apartment—he later made clear—I had invaded. If living with precipitates a living in. The chambre de bonne would echo with teeth grinding at night.

I'd never been able to understand her poems before then, though I'd been introduced to her as a teenager, at which time I developed a strong aversion to the poem "Wild nights – Wild nights!" Now, I'd decided it was another time, and that there must be other poems whose language I could enter. And, only after immersing myself in her language almost completely, reading all of her poems for the first of many times, and within the context of another language, and with a window open onto a courtyard that was being reconstructed, full of scaffolding and smoke, I was able to meet her where she was. In a place "More numerous of Windows," as she says in another poem.

Since then, I've often visited her in the vicinity of openings.

Of Doors

Sometime after, when I was just beginning to write about Emily Dickinson all I wanted to write about was love and death. Write twenty pages about dying, my mentor said. There were no flowers in it. I showed it to him. It's about doors, he said. Write twenty more pages about doors. I wrote twenty more pages about love and death. It's about theater, he said, and I agreed. It was about a door that wouldn't stay shut.

I used to have dreams that this intimacy of writing and revision was a veiled kind of seduction. Then I would wake and shake off those nightly insinuations and spend the weekend in the library while my lover was doing who knows what with whom. Later my mentor married another woman from my class. I don't think he advised her thesis. Revise and re-submit.

Of Vicinities

In 1829, Hitchcock introduced his *Catalogue of Plants Growing Without Cultivation in the Vicinity of Amherst* as surveying an area of roughly "forty or fifty miles," which is roughly the size of San Francisco, where I met my husband, or of Paris, or, by some accounts, of the abandoned land in Detroit, where there are fields of flowers growing without cultivation in the vicinity of city blocks. Driving from California to Massachusetts, we were tourists there. I was pregnant, which was another kind of tourism.

Catalogues of plants growing in the vicinity of somewhere were a feature of the intellectual life of the nineteenth century: of Baltimore, Cincinnati, Columbus, Ottawa, Milwaukee, St. Louis, Salem. Documentation of the vegetation around the vicinity of this other Massachusetts town made up the concluding, anonymous, essay of Elizabeth Peabody's only edition of *Aesthetic Papers*, in which other contributions included Sampson Reed on vegetating "Genius," Emerson on "War," Hawthorne on "Main Street," Thoreau on "Resistance to Civil Government." Peabody was a teacher and a publisher and believed in the innate intelligence of children, their way of uncovering what it is they need to know. Her essay for the edition was called "Language."

The town where I grew up at the end of another century, where I knew the names of at least some of the plants: not even one mile squared. A matter of solitary acres, where we'd walked through the fields pulling Queen Anne's lace in the summer, de-fleecing milkweed in the fall.

Mexico City, where we honeymooned: 500 miles squared. London, where we might have lived had we not already been married: 600. Shiga Prefecture, Japan, where I taught teenagers that reminded me of the ones I'd grown up with, stranded economically within the provincial: 1,550. These are approximations. The Mediterranean: 965,000. The square footage of blue.

Of Marriage

In the spring of 1821, Orra White married Edward Hitchcock in Amherst, Massachusetts. Nearly a decade earlier, on the other side of the Connecticut River, they'd been teachers together. They'd acted side by side together in a play: *Emancipation of Europe, or the Downfall of Bonaparte*. Edward was the playwright. Orra, the Empress of France.

In 1815, the year before what came to be known in some parts of the northwest hemisphere as the Year Without a Summer—they'd begun work on an almanac. In the edition published in 1818, Edward attempted to explain the peculiar alterations in the climate of the summer that had never arrived more than a year before. In Europe, 1816 was the summer Mary Shelley wrote Frankenstein. The sun refused to shine. In Indonesia, a volcano had erupted. Edward thought it might have had something to do with spots on the sun. Orra drew them: gaping black holes.

Now Edward was a minister and Orra was a wife. Shortly after their marriage, in a letter to the scientist Benjamin Silliman, editor of the *American Journal of Science* and professor of chemistry, Edward calls his wife "my Mrs. Colleague." Edward couldn't read the scientific journals in German sent by Silliman, but Orra could translate others, if they were written in French.

A year later, acknowledging receipt of Edward's geological study of the Connecticut River, Orra's accompanying, unauthorized map, Silliman intuits Edward's "coadjutor." He calls the hand of his collaborator "more delicate than yours or mine."

Of Mushrooms

After marriage, but before Amherst, the Hitchcocks move to Conway. There, Edward gathers mushrooms, not for Orra, though she paints them, but for Science, in a small volume one viewer would call "The Honeymoon Album." The Hitchcocks' mushrooms are intimate, quaint. The kind of thing you'd want to own in facsimile if it wasn't already out of print. Together, they sent the mushrooms—picked and painted, once living or never alive—to John Torrey, a chemist and botanist, who had recently helped found the New York Lyceum of Natural History and had even more recently published a *Catalogue of Plants Growing Spontaneously within Thirty Miles of the City of New York*. When they sent him mushrooms, living and dead, Torrey gave the mushrooms numbers, proper names.

Emily Dickinson, fifty years later, from the other side of a Civil War: "The Mushroom is the Elf of Plants –."

Before mushrooms, before Conway, before marriage, Orra had brought the flowers Edward gathered back to the living in delicate paint. The couple likely had also sent Torrey this earlier album, a record of courtship, of plants growing spontaneously in the vicinity of Deerfield. In the herbarium is also demonstration of collaboration between science and art that would evolve into a marriage. During a recent exhibition of Orra White's work, two manuscripts were discovered that reveal Orra and Edward's intellectual transactions in action. The first is Edward's catalogue of the Conway mushrooms, a list that corresponds to Orra's illustrations, disclosing a partnership between representation and classification, coming to see and coming to know. The second is a field sketch of "Prickly Ash and Sweet-Scented Pear," quickly penciled by Orra, annotated by Edward, which another viewer has suggested were mutual contributions to an act of looking and labeling becoming one.

In the painted herbarium, a scientist has penciled, of a plant he does not recognize, "Do send me a specimen."

A mushroom is a small manifestation of an undergirding system. I am not married to a Scientist. How many voyeurs can an authentic partnership sustain?

Of Ministry

"Had Nature an Apostate - / That Mushroom – it is Him!"

After three years in the ministry, Edward left for chemistry, and for Amherst, retiring from the pulpit to join the professoriate. Hitchcock's career as a minister was the same short length, and only half a decade earlier than Ralph Waldo Emerson's would be, whose dead wife and visit to the natural history cabinets at the Jardin des Plantes in Paris confirmed his apostasy. No longer a minister, Emerson devoted his earliest years as a lecturer and essayist to "the greatest delight which the fields and woods minister," "the suggestion of an occult relation between man and the vegetable."

In 1844, the year Emerson published his second series of essays, Edward Hitchcock delivered a lecture on "The Coronation of Winter" at Amherst College. That public talk would become the first in a series he would later publish as *Religious Lectures on Peculiar Phenomena in the Four Seasons*.

Reading Hitchcock's *Religious Lectures* in the fall after I had become a mother, when I found I could no longer write directly about Dickinson; and when, surrounded by scientists for professional reasons, I felt more desperate for the uselessness of language than I ever had before; and as the planet was warming so that California was burning and the snow kept dumping and dumping on Massachusetts all through March; and I was wondering about this technology of close reading I'd been schooled in over decades, what it might become if it was relinquished, out of doors like Higginson's *Out-Door Papers*; and though, like Dickinson, I'd never had and didn't expect to have anything resembling a "saving" experience, I discovered that the concept of ministry made a certain sense to me. Close reading as spiritual survival, oriented toward a vicinity of others.

Hitchcock begins his lecture on winter with saints as scientists, savior as magnifier. These are fit "illustration" of something other than themselves (but see how the catalogue suggests otherwise): the "animal and vegetable world," "the sower going forth to sow," "the vineyards dressed, the grass waving in the fields, the birds flying through the air, the chickens gathering under the wing of their mother, the burrows of the foxes, the plowmen holding the plow, the architect building houses, the soldier going to war, or a band of thieves breaking into the house."

Hitchcock followed his lecture on winter two years later with a lecture on "The Resurrections of Spring." Being a scientist, as well as a minister, he is drawn to the central conundrum of Paul's First Letter to the Corinthians: "How are the dead raised up? And with what body do they come?" What would it mean, materially, to be resurrected, he asks.

Paul's argument is of irresolvable difference: "There is a natural body, and there is a spiritual body," and never the two shall meet. But, according to Hitchcock, Paul bungles the point by getting beautiful with language: a dead body is a seed. And by being a bad scientist.

In Paul's estimation, God gives the seed one body, the stalk of wheat another. As separate as the flesh of "men," "beasts," "fish," "birds," "celestial bodies, and bodies terrestrial," "the sun," "the moon," and the difference between every single glorious star, and every other, burning or waning, explosive in glory. One body is "earthy." The other, post-trumpet, entirely of heaven.

But Hitchcock knows this isn't so. The stalk lies embryonic within the seed's slick case. They are separate, and the same.

In response to the apostle's vagaries, Hitchcock gets botanically particular: seeds aren't dead, though they're "nourished by, the decaying cotyledon. The ascending plumule, making its way to the air, and the descending radicle, spreading in the soil, draw in nourishment from these two sources, and the expanding stalk becomes independent of the seed; and we see in it no resemblance to the seed. Yet that seed was indispensable to its germination."

What the fields and forests minister. "I have great faith in a seed," Thoreau would later write.

Hitchcock not only corrects Paul's poor science; he also argues the apostle should have more faith in his metaphors. It's beautiful to say a body is a seed only if you believe a seed is materially connected to its stalk. Otherwise, why bother. Metaphors reveal material truths yet to be disclosed, a material reminder that knowledge has a horizon.

Hitchcock tries to interpret scripture chemically: a resurrected body reverberates with molecules animating life. An entirely material, and metaphoric, universe: beloved, corpse, bouncy atoms, whatever else.

"They nod to me," Emerson continues, and I nod back.

Of Images

Hitchcock calls the metaphor Paul throws over: a "beautiful illustration." Metaphor feeds on matter just as a fattening caterpillar constructs a chrysalis, emerges victorious, if we project a little beyond the frame.

In the published edition of Edward's collected *Religious Lectures*, winter is the only season without an illustration. An "Element of Blank." Orra has figured the others: summer, autumn, spring.

In her image of spring's resurrections, small lives and their cycles are emblematic, swollen out of proportion to the surrounding scene. A caterpillar the size of a panther slinks fatefully forwards in time toward its rebirth. Below, its transformed body hangs huge above a distant Holyoke Range. In a pond, tadpoles consider a frog that made them, or a frog they'll soon become. A vague yellow bird—a female bobolink?— towers on a branch like one of the giant birds Hitchcock theorized left footprints in what was once soft sand, which later scientists identified as dinosaurs, jogging across now intractable rock. Though the bird is too big, the spindly branch on which it stands erect is static, confident of all that life. In the distance, it is raining or about to rain. A beetle extends its claws. Time stands still and is a circle. The living feed the dead by hand. "Emblems of the Resurrection," the image is called. Caption for all images.

Of Self-Portraits

The same year Hitchcock published his lecture on winter, and Emerson published his essay on "The Poet," Emily Dickinson also published something: she sat for what may be her only image.

Though there may be another—at 33, a grown poet with her arm thrown round a Kate—this first one remains iconic: a lanky teenager with an awkward ribbon around her neck, crooked mouth, wandering eye. In her fingers, flowers. "Morning Glory"? At her elbow on the too-big table, a book. She looks at the photographer, sort of. Fourteen years old.

"I am afraid to own a Body –" begins a later poem. When I was that age, I wanted other bodies before I knew how to organize among them by any category other than want: yellow silk nightgown, dirty brown overalls. Summer nights by Lake George in the Adirondacks, as flowery as Eden. That lake, like Amherst: 40 miles squared.

That poem still bewilders me, because of the generality of its article. A "Body" and "a Soul" could be the speaker's life, or, just as easily, anyone else's: a slave, a lover, or a child ("an unsuspecting Heir –"): any body over which a speaker fears dominion. The problem in the poem isn't ultimately a fear of bodies or of souls, but rather, of "Possession"— from the private "Property" of an "Estate," to the imperial property of a "Frontier." When Dickinson writes, "Possession, not optional –" she is making a "Double" assertion—that a speaker cannot own a body— hers or anyone else's, and that a life nevertheless takes place within "a Body." "Possession" of the basic conditions of life is not possible, and there is no option outside of embodied living. What is the hidden verb that could be a variant for ownership in this poem, eradicating its fear?

Once when someone came to rouse me from a bed in the middle of the night, I told her I was thinking, which was another way, for me, of gratifying a body. Then I lay still in the dark listening to her laughing on the porch with others, kept awake by something abstract. Now, the only thing following her is language.

Dickinson to Higginson: "When Flowers annually died and I was a child, I used to read Dr Hitchcock's Book on the Flowers of North America. This comforted their Absence – assuring me they lived."

Signed: Your Scholar. Elsewhere, Your Gnome.

Of Science

Thomas Wentworth Higginson, in his first essay for *The Atlantic Monthly*, 1858: "the most ignorant person may be a true benefactor to science by forming a cabinet, however scanty, of the animal and vegetable productions of his own township."

The 1850s were the decade when Thoreau began to systematically study the woods and fields around Concord, heading out in early spring to greet particular flowers, day by day, a year later, to the same clearing or hillock or swamp, to see if that orchid was indeed blooming, early or late. This was thirty years after when the Hitchcocks assembled their painted herbaria in the vicinities of Deerfield and Conway. Three decades after when the Amherst Junior Class published Hitchcock's *Catalogue* as a local point of reference for the more extensive "Floras, Compendiums, and Manuals of American Plants" that were beginning to come into print.

When Thoreau met his orchid, he cross-referenced his own observations with local catalogues by Jacob Bigelow, whose Amherst was Boston, Alphonso Wood and Almira Lincoln Phelps whose Boston was upstate and eastern New York, and eventually, Asa Gray, who, along with John Torrey, consolidated American botany, sent collectors to the edges of the continent, and extended the vicinity to the globe.

Before all this, European science in the States—though it still scarcely knew what haunted its localities—had intentions that extended far beyond the local.

When Thomas Jefferson, president from 1801-1809, organized the Lewis and Clark expedition, an eighteenth-century equivalent to a 1969 NASA expedition to the moon, his intentions, like Nixon's, were nationalistic, imperial. Jefferson commanded his explorers, for the sake of science, to collect, especially, specimens of anything particularly massive or grand. Jefferson sent such findings—a moose skeleton, for example—directly to France, c/o the Compte de Buffon, whose theories of biological and moral decay in the New World prompted even an inveterate regionalist like Jefferson to become continental in consciousness.

Before Jefferson, the Bartrams. After them, Gray. These men gathered plants to see how big their country was, or could be, how much it could stand to profit from itself.

Of Star

Emily Dickinson studied science, but she was also skeptical of its reach. She read Hitchcock in the winter and used Almira Lincoln Phelps's *Familiar Lectures on Botany* at school. Her family owned books on anatomy and chemistry. She writes poems about explosions, volcanic and otherwise. She assembled a not-especially scientific herbarium around the same time she sat for that self-portrait. The portrait is gray. The flowers, still, some of them: yellow or pink.

The fact that Dickinson was touched by a popular interest in science that permeated her age has attracted so much attention, though, because in our age, a lot of different kinds of knowledge, and especially forms of knowledge more lucrative than the literary, have ended up clumped together within the scientific. But science is not a sufficient justification now or then for the making of and especially not the study of such non-utilitarian things as poems.

As much as Dickinson was a very bad Christian, and her poetry is unimaginable without the constraints of Christianity, so did she put little faith in science, though her poetry is a species of scientific method, lurching against the confines of the known.

"'Arcturus' is his other name – / I'd rather call him 'Star.' / It's very mean of Science / To go and interfere!"

Dickinson was caught up in science, and sentimentalism, the way we are caught up in global capital. The way the internet lays piping in the brain. Physics has both a utilitarian and a non-utilitarian face. Nuclear weapons and dark matter. Poems are too embroiled within vicinity to track in either/or.

Of Massachusetts

Edward Hitchcock published his *Report on the Geology, Mineralogy, Botany, and Zoology of Massachusetts* in 1833. This led to a commission, by the legislature, to lead a team of naturalists to enumerate and describe all other nonhuman things that were known to be living or dead in the Commonwealth.

For his naturalists, Hitchcock recruited men whose means and interests had allowed them to study their most immediate place. Like Gilbert White on the other side of the Atlantic, whose late-eighteenth-century *Natural History of Selbourne* marks the beginning of what we have come to call, since Thoreau, "nature writing," many of these men, like Hitchcock, like Emerson, were ministers. Their attention to seashells or vegetables was a way of locating other living and nonliving ministers, outside pulpits, outside books.

Tasked with the invertebrates of Massachusetts, in 1841, Augustus Gould writes of "true *barnacles*": "These shells, though everywhere common, seem to be regarded everywhere as strangers. They are Jews among other shells."

Of Extinction

In 1840, Ebenezer Emmons writes: "This remarkable animal"—the beaver—"is probably driven entirely from the bounds of Massachusetts. It has become, like some other animals, extinct, and is known only in historical records as having formerly been a tenant of our waters."

"The Moose is not found at present within the limits of this State, neither has it probably been taken within its bounds for the last thirty or forty years. It may, therefore, be considered as extinct, as far as Massachusetts is concerned."

"Whether the Caribou was ever an inhabitant of this State, is now difficult to determine. Civilization we know early drove away the more shy and timid animals."

Other quadrupeds absent from Massachusetts in 1840: the common wolf, the American lion, signs of any species of bear.

The long nineteenth century was an important century in the history of the expansion of time. Lyell, Darwin: the slow time scales of geological history, the immediacy of the struggle for existence writ long and lasting through that slowness of evolutionary time. These scientists reoriented earthly existence to the scale of strata, the impossible pacing of the development of the seeing eye.

The long nineteenth century also saw the not so gradual demise of species that, not so long before, had seemed to sum up the magnitude and abundance of a new world. Though that magnitude and abundance was itself an illusion: a population boom of plant and animal species after the decimation of Indigenous human populations that had lived in vicinity with these other lives for many thousands of years.

In the lumbering histories of the Earth and its inhabitants that Lyell and Darwin popularized within the century in which they lived, extinction was a burr in the elegant elongations of gradual change. If all things were slow, this should be slow, too. But the distance between fossils and lives sometimes suggests otherwise. Lyell and Darwin were anti-catastrophes. But extinction, particularly when asteroids or humans are involved, can be catastrophic: a battering, hunt, to the end.

Of Scale

Orra illustrated nearly all of her husband's scientific works: from large-scale classroom drawings of what Hitchcock thought were fossilized footprints of birds, extinct Mastodons, and the volcanic surface of the Earth, to reproducible lithographs of shells and striated rock for textbooks.

His lecture on winter, which, as we have seen, she did not illustrate, describes in minute detail the effects of a singular meteorological event: a messy snow and rain storm, which, through slight gradations of temperature, precipitation shifting from snow to rain to ice, transformed the world, that is the vicinity of Amherst, for a full week and a half into a "magnificent temple," a "fairy land" of glittering forms, trees and grass, rigid in icy rigor, casting "prismatic colors," "splendid sapphire blue," "amethystine purple," "intense topaz yellow," "sea green beryl," "rich emerald green." Precious jewels and adjectives, Hitchcock's winter scene ends in a "deep hyacinth red," some glint of the bloody living, reasserting itself amidst all this lifeless splendor.

Edward reckoned it "among the unique revelations of nature."

Hyperboles like these can only be achieved when the scope of a viewer's experience has been relatively local in scale. "The Natural Bridge" of Rockbridge County, wrote Thomas Jefferson in his *Notes on the State of Virginia*, "the most sublime of Nature's works." Jefferson may have been to Paris, but he knew nothing of the Himalayas, not to mention, the Grand Canyon.

Hitchcock hedges. "To those who have not witnessed" this particular storm, "I may seem enthusiastic and extravagant in my estimates." Prior to this storm, he also would have had trouble believing his own descriptions. But the storm changes everything. The local goes "celestial."

Of New York

If you grow up in New York outside of New York City, you can't tell people that you're from New York the way other people are from Massachusetts, or California, or Michigan. They assume you mean something other. So you need to qualify: upstate, or, from the State of. I'm from a place that likely no one reading this will recognize or remember. Growing up there, I always had the feeling that swaths of the State had been left behind in time. Still playing the same pop songs thirty years later. And all that farmland. All that whiteness. And those graying barns.

Though the State of also has its own neglected beauties. There are hills there, too, that might be allegories. And a river, an orchard, a cemetery, and a village of vinyl-sided homes. I wouldn't call it Eden, but it resembles so many other places in this country, where no one leaves, and no one goes. "I'm Nobody! Who are you? / Are you Nobody, too?" Of all the poems of Dickinson's I've taught, this one never fails to produce a surprisingly personal response.

Of Education

Hitchcock credited Amos Eaton for his initial interest in botany. Before that, he'd been more interested in stars. He'd ruined his eyes chasing a comet. Later, Hitchcock's attention would turn toward a meeting of the inorganic and organic: fossils, and the long, slow life of rocks. The study of botany corresponds to a developmental period in his career, when he was most caught up with students—first at Deerfield Academy, and later at Amherst. And with the early years of his relationship with Orra.

Hitchcock eventually became successful as both a scientist and an educator. Eaton was more influential as an educator than a scientist. Along with his former student, Almira Lincoln Phelps, Eaton established a robust program of botanical field study for young students, including women, around Troy, New York, where I went to high school. Phelps would later teach at the school I attended. It was there that she authored *Familiar Lectures on Botany*, which Dickinson, in conjunction with Hitchcock's textbook, *Elementary Geology*, used at Amherst Academy.

In addition to botany, Dickinson studied Latin, Greek, German, chemistry, math. I studied biology, chemistry, physics. English and French. European and American History. Dante's *Divine Comedy*. Emily Dickinson's poems. We did not study botany, though we did watch, in one class, a lurid film called *Sexual Encounters of the Floral Kind*. This was ostensibly about insects fertilizing flowers, but the music and close-ups suggested otherwise and were exacerbated by the dynamics of our classroom—male science teacher, crowd of teenage girls. Vaginal close-ups of an orchid. Wasps and figs.

In another class, I wanted to read and write outside. Not today, the teacher said. You have Dionysian tendencies, but an education is Apollonian.

So I never studied the plants where I grew up. In 1816, Hitchcock attended a lecture by Eaton on the practice of botany. The following summer, Hitchcock, along with Dennis Cooley, who later became a botanist and moved to the Midwest, and the local doctor, Stephen Williams, began a comprehensive study of plants growing in the vicinity of Deerfield. Williams compiled an herbarium of local specimens—an album of dried and pressed plants—with a particular emphasis on plants with medicinal properties. Included in that herbarium are illustrations by Williams's wife, Harriet Goodhue, a former student of Orra White's.

Many of Goodhue's botanical illustrations are copies of Orra's. I called the herbarium she painted of the plants gathered by Edward in the vicinity of Deerfield a documentation of courtship. Like all courtships, the Hitchcock's herbarium combines liveliness and convention. Though the majority of the figures are original, drawn either from life or from a life very recently suspended, some are copies themselves, of British botanical illustrations. The gorgeous, deadly *Digitalis* for instance, is elegantly pilfered from the frontispiece of William Withering's *An Account of the Foxglove*, published in England in the years immediately following the Revolutionary War.

The herbarium reveals Orra's deep knowledge and attention to plantlife, living and dead, in the field and on the page, at a hyper-local level, and her participation in aesthetic systems of representing the natural world that were, in an age of European imperialism, all but planetary in scale, and horrifying in consequence.

Of Deer/Forests/Bobolinks/Wolves/Flowers/Deer

In the decades surrounding either side of the Civil War, there were no white-tailed deer living in eastern Massachusetts, no Canadian geese, no beavers flooding the woods. Think of it: Thoreau never saw a deer near Walden. Never saw a beaver.

It's difficult to say what percentage of the area that now makes up the state was forested prior to European settlement. Indigenous Americans had altered and maintained the land and its living plants and animals through cultivation and by controlled fires for centuries. By 1850, forests covered less than 30% of the state. In the latter half of the nineteenth century, farmers got wind of a place called Ohio, a land blessed with fewer rocks, and Europe was once again moving west. Settlers who stayed in the east clustered closer to textile mills, shipping hubs, industry or universities. The forests filled back in. In 2017, the state is 62% forest, one of the country's ten most forested states.

As forests came back, however, birds of open pasture, like meadow-larks, swallows, bobolinks, receded.

In a poem from the 1870s, Dickinson reports on the bobolink as "Extrinsic to Attention," as already, always disappearing: its vicinity always already vacated of song. Where does song go when it has nowhere or everywhere to go, when it doesn't know the vicinities from which it sucks? "Often I am permitted to return to a meadow," the poet Robert Duncan would later write of the practice of poetry. When Dickinson's "Bird of Birds is gone," he "Nullif[ies] the Meadow" in his wake.

The comings and goings of plant and animal species as the result of habitat transformation due to human population expansion and migration across the span of the nineteenth century are on a different scale from the catastrophic endings that mark the terminus of a species. In some parts of the States of, far from Massachusetts, in the opening decades of the twenty-first century, populations of gray wolves are on the rise. Nevertheless, these lives and deaths, some of them only a temporary coming or going, extinction within vicinity, are also the result of anthropogenic change. In the States of, living beings move from state to state to state.

In some parts of Massachusetts, the deer are so plentiful that the flowers Thoreau visited won't grow. The deer maintain the landscape now, populating it with what they won't eat. The woods around Concord at the beginning of the twenty-first century: a desert of huckleberries and pine. I walked through them, carrying a child on my back.

Of Lilies

One June, congratulating a neighbor on the birth of a child, Dickinson wrote: "Let me command to Baby's attention the only Commandment I ever obeyed – 'Consider the Lilies.'"

And she really did. She used to stay up late in the winter to make sure her hothouse flowers survived the night, conservatory windows opened inward and the charcoal stove glowing. And what is all lawn now was all garden then: daylilies, oriental lilies, lilies of the valley. Before she began tending to them as children, she studied them.

In her *Familiar Lectures on Botany*, Almira Lincoln Phelps advocates for the moral effects of botanizing as a youth: "By attention to the vegetable structure, you will, doubtless, be induced to think more upon the wonderful mechanism of your own material frames; upon the analogy," she elaborates, "and yet infinite difference," she clarifies, "between yourselves and the lilies of the field."

But, like much else at school, especially regarding religion, even tempered with science, Dickinson willfully revised this lesson. She was lily-like, too, she thought.

Remember those daylilies she handed to Higginson in August. An "introduction." A gesture Higginson found childish: sentimental, and willfully indirect. A decade later, in the spring, to Mrs. Holland, she wrote: "Please 'consider' me – An antique request," but one renewed by spring.

Dickinson's practice was founded on that consideration, of how a poet, nourished on the water, dirt, sun of a unique locality, and on Romantic philosophy that had crossed a sea, along with enthusiasms for the scientific that were pervasive and catching on more than two sides of the Atlantic, could be lily-like, a "vegetable genius," unfurling like a scroll, or opening like a perfumed fist, or snapping shut like tiger's teeth—calla, nymphaea, stargazer—a new Stella de Ora every other day. More fragrant than Keats's "leaves to a tree," but just as easy.

Elsewhere, she relates lilies to the materiality of books, as when, in a note to Mary Bowles, she moves from an observation—"Even the 'Lilies of the field' have their dignities"—to a question about the book's casing—"Why did you bind it in green and gold? / The *immortal* colors," the colors of the album Dickinson bound her herbarium in, and the cover of Whitman's first, anonymous, *Leaves of Grass*.

At another moment, Dickinson elides all these analogies—between lilies and humans, and lilies and books—thanking Mrs. Sweetser for "'considering the Lilies,'" before comparing these to herself and her friend. "The Bible must have had us in mind, when it gave that liquid Commandment." Later, complimenting her friend's "account of Lilies," she writes: it was "so fresh I could almost pick them." By the time he was editing her poems and introducing them to the world, Higginson described Dickinson's poems as "torn up by the roots, with rain and dew and earth still clinging."

Claiming a literal affinity between the living and the literary was a common trope of the age. Whitman never tired of it, revising his poems into grass. But a metaphor is also, as Dickinson puts it, a "liquid commandment." The earthliness rinses off.

Considering lilies, as Phelps advises, leads students toward the similitudes between plants and persons, and, at the same time, that a child is not at all the same as a plant. In its fissures, a metaphor, like an education, is incomplete.

The lily dwells, and learns, in dirt—"Through the Dark Sod – as Education –"—her confidence confirming one of many radical differences between students and plants, at least as Dickinson understood each. "Afterward – in the Meadow, / Swinging her Beryl Bell –," the lily needn't look forward or back: "The Mold-life – all forgotten – now." Whereas Dickinson's poetics never forget the Mold.

When Dickinson imagines her self becoming plant, that consideration is driven by a sense that grasses, daisies, lilies do not face "all these problems of the dust." Lilies, at least in the vicinity of Amherst, are perennial, renewing themselves each year, educated out of the bulb, then prolonged by that buried part of themselves. So, in considering lilies, we learn that, like us, they know color and music and "Extasy," and, unlike us, they are entirely responsible for their own resurrections. Though, like a lily, I have learned that an "Education" can sometimes be a way of bringing oneself back to life.

Of Metaphor and Prose

Hitchcock's lecture on the resurrected body, on spring, begins with a passage from Corinthians. When Dickinson turns to the same passage, she takes up only the moldering side, counteracting it with *"this"*: "'Sown in dishonor'! / Ah, Indeed! / May *this* 'dishonor' be?"

Dickinson's "this" is outside the poem, and is the poem, a pointing that points at itself. To be a seed is "fine." Just as now, there was a historical predicament that required poems to be arguments at times. Then, it was a Great Awakening. Her friends and her family woke up. She did not want to be awake in that way. Reader, you know what it is for us.

Dickinson kept "Sabbath" "at Home - / With a Bobolink – for a Chorister – / And an Orchard – for a Dome –." A lyricist whose recalcitrant church-shirking anticipates Wallace Stevens's much belated Modernist "Sunday Morning," with its imported oranges and cockatoo in the sun.

If part of Hitchcock's difficulty with Corinthians is that Paul veers precipitously toward poetry, but then, by bad science, misses the poetics of the material world, for Dickinson, the "Apostle is askew," because "Corinthians I.15. narrates / A circumstance or two."

This is the poet for whom poetry was "A fairer House than Prose –." For whom "Prose" was a punishing "Closet," designed to "still" the body but failing to "Still!" the "Brain." Can prose only ever do that: convey a "circumstance or two," bound by causality, this then that? There are forms of prose I feel shut up in, but luckily one of the benefits of prose is its puncturability. Like poetry, it can, at times, be relational. Its fine dishonor could be its love for the Earth.

Of Houses

In a letter to Higginson in the spring of 1876, Dickinson reworked a line from Paul's other letter to the Corinthians, converting biblical prose to her own characteristic common meter:

"The House not made with Hands" it was –
Thrown open wide to me –

In Corinthians, this "house not made with hands, eternal in the heavens" is a reminder of the ephemerality of "our earthly house," with all its earthly things, including the body. Embodiment gets in the way of being with god, and so, Paul writes, we should be "willing [...] to be absent from the body," in order "to be present with the Lord."

The desire to be judged to have used our bodies well enough to settle them into this handless house forever should direct what we labor at on Earth. Longed-for house, glistening in the blinding light of the future, which is like the light off the Pacific, while we muck about here, trying to keep ourselves as free of smuttiness as possible, awaiting eternity. I hope you realize, as with much else here, I am internalizing the zeitgeist of Dickinson's era, not my own beliefs.

Dickinson, however, casts her easeful entry there, into the past: this house "was," she writes, already "Thrown open wide to me." She then revises what Paul suggests are painful Earthly labors—"we groan," he writes—into a hunt for flowers.

"I had long heard of an Orchis before I found one, when a child," she reports; "but the first clutch of the stem is as vivid now, as the Bog that bore it." Before and after blur around the preposition "of": hearing "of" a phantom Orchis elides into a clutching "of" it in some present all subsiding within the context "of" a remembered Bog.

Dickinson calls this transference between time and place, between idea and thing, then and now, Orchis and Bog, "transport," a term she uses elsewhere to describe the unknowability of the experience of flowers—"whose suspense or transport may surpass [our] own"—and the difficulty in defining their effects—"Half a transport – half a trouble –"—on those that live with them.

When she wrote this letter, she had been reading Higginson's essays for decades. He also wrote of bogs.

When she concludes by telling Higginson, "Though inaudible to you, I have long thanked you," she further toys with Corinthians (and with Higginson, and perhaps even herself). Whatever god is, it can't know us, "whether absent or present," though we labor to be known by it. Linking her experience of reading orchids in Higginson to the continuing vivacity of locating one in memory places her "Preceptor" in this position of distant deity: the kind of deity she would recognize. When she tells Higginson, "I do not leave my Father's House," she means, also, the heavenly house is already mine own.

I bring this up because, though I have never lived in the vicinity of Amherst, I have looked for the flowers Dickinson conjures in her poems in the hills around Amherst. I have arrived late to *Epigaea repens*, pinkening past snow. And I have cupped a Quaker lady in my hands. The dominant notion of an intellectual life, now, is that it might be lived anywhere. So "The Brain – is wider than the Sky –" and flits from state to state. But that has not been my experience of what it means to think, or live, in or of vicinities.

Dickinson's letter refigures the relation between earthliness and eternity. Gathering a flower throws "wide" the doors of an otherworldly house to a girl with her ankles sunk in a bog, or a woman with her cursor poised for recollection.

"I dwell in Possibility" is a poem about that "House." See-through "Roof" whose "Gambrels" open directly to "the Sky." There, labor gathers. "Hands" are "narrow." A simple effort abundant enough to resurrect "Paradise" as Earth. As I revise this, the spent narcissus I force inside each winter are tipping into the window frame. The room is still, and humming, and full of green and books and traces of those with whom I share a life. Webs in the corners. A red bead. Silent records and instruments waiting to be spun or touched.

If, in this poem, Dickinson relates heaven's house to "Prose," contrasting its frame to earthly "Possibility," she revisits that formulation in a poem written in the same year she writes to Higginson of bogs and orchids: "Gathered into the Earth / And out of story –." An equation that sets narrative in heaven, preserving poetry for Earth. In that poem, too, gathering, again, is the operative verb.

Of Florida

Florida is a place that hasn't yet appeared in this vicinity. My husband is from Florida. In the north, it's a place of pine-barrens and lovely punks. Sink holes. Springs you can swim in in the winter. There isn't a huge diversity of plants, so it's possible to know them. Palmetto, dogwood, magnolia. Another living oak.

Once when we were visiting, we went on a tour of the writer Marjorie Kinnan Rawlings' house, author of *The Yearling* and other regionalist works. She'd come to Florida from the Midwest in the 1920s with her husband and when she saw this particular orange grove, she knew she'd discovered "her place on Earth." The tour guide kept saying this, "her place on Earth," in a gentle not-quite Southern accent, as we wandered through the house, admiring the wicker furniture, learning about the failure of her marriage, taking turns carrying and bouncing our child to sleep. There were chickens in the yard and alligators in the river. I don't think I'll ever find that place, I remember thinking, any place on Earth I'd know well enough to think of as "my own."

Of California

My husband came with me to Massachusetts from California for a temporary job at a university there. Now, we're moving back to California so that he can continue the old job he left off: advising others on the use of their land. Forest fires, mud slides, and gazebos in neighbors' yards. Before we left, there was an oil spill, up the coast. Climate change feels more present in the West. I won't water the flowers I fell over myself this spring and summer admiring in other people's yards. In fact, I won't grow them there at all. "The Lilac is an ancient shrub," but so much in California is dry or forgotten, except for the hills, and the allegories, and the sea, and anyway, a California lilac is a Ceanothus.

I'm not sure how I feel about moving back. Moving anywhere. Moving at all. I'd like to commit to a vicinity, wherever and whatever it is. In an interview, the poet Robert Hass says that he felt it was important to put the names of California things—animals, plants—into his poems because other poets weren't, pretending New England was England, with its neat seasons, and its winter that isn't really winter at all. Gertrude Stein and Robert Frost lived in Oakland when they were young, but you'd never know it by her repetitions, or his birches.

It isn't that I don't like California. It's just that, after nearly a decade, I still don't know the names of things growing along roadsides there, apart from the obvious. Yucca shooting upward into a white effusion I thought had a name in Spanish having to do with wedding dresses, but when I looked it up just now in the *Introduction to California Spring Wildflowers*, which was a wedding present, I see that its common name is "The Lord's Candle." The things we do for love.

And anyway, the poet Linda Gregg once told the poet Robert Hass (I read about this in the poet Harryette Mullen's introduction to the book of tankas she wrote while walking through the vicinities of Los Angeles, a city that is nothing if not vicinities of): that's not how anyone sees the world. We see the common pink-purple fringy splendor over yonder. Rather than the sticky monkey flower—mimulus—I planted this year in my garden.

Of Friendship/Marriage/Majesty/Papers/Flowers/Absence/Scholarship

In the likely winter of 1877, Emily Dickinson to Thomas Wentworth Higginson: "Dear friend. Thank you for the permission to write Mrs Higginson. / Often, when troubled by entreaty, that paragraph of your's has saved me – 'Such being the Majesty of the Art you presume to practice, you can at least take time before dishonoring it' // I recently found two Papers of your's that were unknown to me, and wondered anew at your withdrawing Thought so sought by others. When Flowers annually died and I was a child, I used to read Dr Hitchcock's Book on the Flowers of North America. This comforted their Absence – assuring me they lived. /// Your Scholar –"

Of Acquaintance

Higginson, in *The Atlantic Monthly*, in the fall of 1861: "Even the driest and barest book of Natural History is good and nutritious, so far as it goes, if it represents genuine acquaintance; one can find summer in January by pouring over the Latin catalogues of Massachusetts plants and animals in Hitchcock's Report."

Emily Dickinson to Mrs. T.W. Higginson, summer 1876: "////// You perhaps sleep as I write, for it is now late, and I give you Good night with fictitious lips, for to me you have no Face. 'We thank thee Oh Father' for these strange Minds, that enamor us against thee."

It is not possible to know the persons an author loves. But apparently, it is possible to write to them. I never cared for the faceless dolls, the ones whose outward demeanors, along with their inner lives, you were supposed to imagine. But a reader also apparently has no face.

Of Companionship

What would it mean for one book to be a companion to another? I wrote one book, then I revisited it until it became something else entirely. Hitchcock's *Catalogue of Plants Growing in the Vicinity of* was revisited years later by the antiquarian and lichenologist Edward Tuckerman, brother of the poet Frederick Goddard Tuckerman, who lived and wrote poems in the vicinity of Dickinson, acquaintance of Thomas Wentworth Higginson, with whom he used to go on flower walks in the vicinity of Cambridge. Tuckerman, who had Coleridge open on his study table, and the door to this study open. Who expanded Hitchcock's list. Who admired the humility of lichen, but wouldn't project the symbiotic companionship (algae and fungi) later scientists argued for onto this organism.

When I write about Amherst, am I writing about Schuylerville, or Bernal Hill, or other low mountains I have climbed? When I write of another marriage, am I commenting on the invisible tendons of my own?

How a body disappears within a pronoun. There was a real woman whose fullness was not recorded. Who didn't like the look of the fineness of her lines projected onto the largeness of a classroom wall. Whose botanical drawings—scaled up, for his lectures—have been lost to time. There is a man I know who writes music, only to let it disappear into a day.

Of Springtime

Orra, born in Amherst, May 1793.

Orra did not write much, so what we have of her are images of things other than herself.

The majority of her children, born in March or in May.

Of the eight born, five live.

Her respective age in the years of their births: almost 29, 31, not quite 33, almost exactly 35, not quite 39, 40, 43, 45.

I will be 38 when this book finds its way into the opposite of winter.

The Hitchcocks, married May 31, 1821.

May 4, 1855: Orra suffers a major fall and ails for the rest of her life. May 26, 1863: after almost 42 years of marriage, Orra dies in Amherst and is buried there.

Spring was a major season in her time on Earth.

Of Of

Prepositions have no feeling. There is no feeling of of, the way William James thought conjunctions had feelings: and, if, but, by, as palpable as cold or blue. The feeling of conjunctions comes from their embodiment. Ligaments of prose: connecting cause and effect, shoring up clauses, binding after to before. So, Dickinson's Lily completes her education around a conjunctive "Afterwards," linking stanza to stanza, precipitating a move from "Mold-life" to the ecstatic "Beryl Bell," green or pink, of lilies of the valley.

In its emptiness and association, of is absorbent rather than connective. Yet, a preposition can distinguish between conditions of belonging as subtle and stark as belonging to a place, but not being of it. The way Puritans defined their place on Earth; the way my Quaker father once defined prayer for me as a teenager, which is all that Quakers do. Absenting while being with and in. Off with that nothingness while trees rustle and seasons are unconciliatory. To be aligned by preposition, rather than conjunction, is to be bound by supposition rather than injunction: to be possibly in the vicinity of, rather than required to proceed.

For instance, I've long loved the way of and for follow each other through Dickinson's "House" of "Possibility":

> More numerous *of* Windows –
> Superior – *for* Doors –
>
> *Of* Chambers as the Cedars –
> Impregnable *of* eye –
> And *for* an everlasting Roof
> The Gambrels *of* the Sky –
>
> *Of* Visitors – the fairest –
> *For* Occupation – This

This *this.* I will not lead you through a closer and closer reading. I don't believe that closeness translates well to prose. Notice, nonetheless, the opening and closing of doors and windows, indirections of belonging, of or for, how they render the edges of place on Earth, with its Italianate stanzas, diaphanous, how permeable it becomes not only to actions of attention, but also to what is living and dying outside, "of […] the Cedars," and "of the Sky."

IMAGINING
MOTHERING

1.

A friend says motherhood is like living with your heart outside your body. This is more like science fiction than at first it seems I decide days after we've talked.

Imagination makes unavailable bodies visible, but only inwardly. Motherhood puts a body into the world. Motherhood therefore makes imagination real, while also—I don't know if this is true, I'm following the thoughts of my friend—making bodies both more real and more imaginary, a body that can live without a heart.

Later, I'll learn: there it is, in my arms, in the empty branches, bird, bird, bird, responding to that alien starling, I look after you, following your senses beyond what I see.

It's somewhere in that emptiness, and in ears, a thrumming, cry.

2.

In an essay on why Søren Kierkegaard abandoned his fiancée, Regine Olsen, rejecting a life of homely pleasures for a life of intellectual charades, György Lukács writes, "die werkliche Frau, die Mütter," has no longing for infinity. Her longing stops at Earth.

I read this essay one spring years before becoming a mother, in the throes of one of the most important friendships of my life. The person I had become so friendly with had lived in a city by the sea for ten years without ever seeing waves break themselves along Ocean Beach. There was hardly any furniture in his small apartment. There was a desk.

We lay on the floor, arguing. The essay thumbtacked above the desk.

Through the window to the left of some true mother, plum trees, dark branches and pale air smattering with obtrusive purple.

3.

One fall after becoming a mother, I read all of Emily Dickinson's letters straight through as if they were a novel or some other force of direction that required thoroughness from beginning to end. Dickinson did never become a mother. She was not a novelist, though she called one novelist, "my George Eliot."

To a friend, she writes, "our first Neighbor, our Mother." Elsewhere, in a poem, she writes of "A Vastness, as a Neighbor" that does not become, but comes, like "A Wisdom without Face or Name." Distances within, among.

Note the imprecision of the article preceding Wisdom, if you would be my mother or my student, gentle reader.

4.

Before becoming a mother, I was sometimes a teacher. Women have long dominated teaching as a profession in the United States. Particularly since the reform movements beginning in the nineteenth century, as schools became more democratic, and the purpose of schooling began to be understood as the creation of well-informed citizens, rather than the reproduction of an elite, women were seen as ideal teachers because of their moral rather than their intellectual aptitude. Teaching was an extension of their work within the home.

When I teach, I try to create an atmosphere of polite, rather than passionate, friendship. I participate with my students as a student, but I am also always a little remote. My mother is a little like this: always the first to get off the phone.

I sometimes begin classes by asking students to tell the story of their names. Once, when I was teaching a class for teachers, I wrote:

My mother knew my name before she knew me. I find this hard to imagine.

Instead, I imagine a nameless, human, absence I could hold in my arms. I'd carry it up a mountain, across a lake in a canoe, into the back of lecture halls and poetry readings on rainy nights in New York, like the baby at the Robert Creeley reading I only remember because the poet stopped in the middle of the poem to babble along, all the places you shouldn't take a small, nameless human, for fear that it will force others to notice it, and with it, you. I don't remember the baby, or the baby's mother, or the poem. Only that there was a pause. And that outside, it was raining.

Although I can't imagine motherhood, I imagine that motherhood might demand faculties other than, or in addition to, the imagination.

Teaching didn't prepare me to become a mother, but teaching, like mothering, like friendship, initiates a thinking with and in response that is in real-time, different from reading or delving in an archive, evolving, yet not yet narrative. Teaching is not a surrogacy for motherhood. Mothering is itself a kind of surrogacy. Your child, never yours alone.

5.

I imagined I would carefully document a pregnancy, ministering to all that possibility with acute attention, writing it down.

In the lonely anxieties of a first trimester, I do find some calm in writing the beginnings of letters to an unimaginable child. But this writing isn't about expansion—it doesn't come from a place of new knowledge or authority, or from the terror of miscarriage or the alienation of not saying what it is I am now always thinking—but from being inhabited by the unknown and the realization that this "Wisdom without Face or Name" is within me, and is not me. As a mother, I am already becoming uncanny. Such a body, and yet not singly a body at all.

Later on, pregnancy becomes almost the exact inverse of this, since one of its peculiarities, once world begins to see through your body to your secret, is the overwhelming approval that greets you from almost every corner of life: strangers, neighbors, mothers, friends. The entire human species seems suddenly invested in your visible signal that you will contribute to its survival. I was congratulated while stretching at rest stops off the highway in South Dakota, while waddling across the street in New York. I found it suddenly less difficult to talk to my mother, or my husband's mother, or the neighbor down the hall.

We live in a country that so dogmatically approves of pregnancy that its present chosen leader threatens to "punish" women who, when facing the true terror it is to "give" a life that was never yours to give, might choose to dial back life's relentless love of itself, to return to the slightly more certain condition of being singular, to arrest a doubling. The overwhelming approval with which we welcome reproduction masks the true peculiarity and privacy of motherhood, whose darkness is at first within, and later, between. And so, despite all its later visibility, there is an attendant privacy to even those later months, and to the years to come. The two of you, and neither/nor.

6.

Meanwhile, an ultrasound puts an end to the imagination. The first time we see our child, she/he/it is an alien fish cast out of outer space.

The technician thinks we'd like 3D. My insides turn from dark to artificial pink as this being goes shifting in and out of light. Measurements and assessments. I wait to be told that there is nothing to imagine so I can go out into California and imagine two-dimensional things.

We tell the technician we don't want the images of our child-to-be. But he's insistent. We should show this one, he says, drawing a circle around genitals, on prom night. Children love to see their selves before they had a self, he says.

I add this stack of folded images to the even more foreign ones of eight weeks ago. I make a little pile on top of a bookshelf and cover it with books. To throw away the images would seem inauspicious. But I don't want what they claim to know.

Too real, and yet unrealized. Too dark, and yet too pink.

7.

I began to really imagine motherhood when teaching an essay by John Berger called "Ape Theater," in which his mother quietly dies.

When she first appears in the opening paragraphs, Berger's mother is largely an aside. The essay begins with the visits to the zoo Berger made with both his parents as a child. His mother didn't like to go, but when she did, she would sometimes visit the bears. Berger and his father preferred the apes. "I can see now," Berger writes long after her death, why she didn't want to witness the distilled violence of chimpanzees and gorillas, "the passions which lead to the spilling of blood." As a boy, this essayist spends a lot of time staring at monkeys through bars.

Then his mother disappears, replaced by four pages on the melancholy of evolution's long time scales and the differences and proximities between humans and apes.

When his mother returns, she is first a kind of "thought," and then quickly thereafter, on the same page, a ghost.

"My mother used to say," Berger swerves in the middle of a paragraph that begins by reflecting on how apes, like humans, are "partly victims of their own bodies," scrounging about in each other's fur looking for fleas to exterminate. "But it goes further than Mother thought," Berger amends. For primates, grooming is not only about hygiene, not only about the complaints of having a body. It's also about pleasure, the surplus of what a body can do.

Berger's correction of his mother is not only a correction of her thinking about bodies, but also a correction of bodies themselves as dutiful or predictable. It goes further than "Mother thought," and it goes further than what any of us think about mothers, especially when it comes to what they may be thinking and what their bodies may be doing.

Berger, perhaps like a mother himself, is a master of withholding. Before the reader can hound him about the obliquity of these connections, he's back to evolution! How apes evolved to use their arms more than other animals, by reaching for "fruit at the ends of branches!"

When next we see his mother (in the very next, this jolting, paragraph), she is flanked on either side by natural selection:

> I must have been two years old when I had my first cuddly toy. It was a monkey. A chimpanzee, in fact. I think I called him Jackie. To be certain, I'd have to ask my mother. She would remember. But my mother is dead. There is just a chance—one in a hundred million (about the same as a chance mutation being favoured by natural selection)—that a reader may be able to tell me, for we had visitors to our home in Highams Park, in East London, sixty years

ago, and I presented my chimp to everyone who came through the front door. I think his name was Jackie.

As a reader, in no relation to Berger (my mother may not even have been born sixty years before the composition of this essay, and in any case, she had never left North America until I was 18 and she came to France), I find the pathos of this paragraph almost over-powering.

After correcting his mother, after going on to demonstrate his very grown-up authorial prowess, yoking together the tactile details of observation in the present—the apes and their swinging limbs, gesturing hands—to the grandiose sweep of evolutionary time, the author exposes himself as once again, and perhaps even now, an anxious child, a very small child indeed, too young for the zoo, clutching a toy.

One of the essay's ostensible subjects—evolutionary time—is sequestered within parentheses, while a single, wavering, childhood memory expands to momentarily distract the author from his purpose. Within this space, the kinds of certainty that drive essays, that carry them long enough in one direction to arrive at some place other than where they started, breaks down. Material conditions render imagination out of place. To be certain, Berger must ask his mother. But his mother is dead.

This is the only mention of his mother's death, and the last time she appears, in the essay. Berger's turn to the reader in the wake of this confession is not a chummy Victorian aside—"Reader, I loved"—but a frantic pawing after what a reader might possibly know or not know, how intimately the lives of readers and writers, children and mothers, may or may not be entwined.

Could you, reader, take the place of my mother, affirm that slight, vulnerable knowledge that remains her dominion and that has disappeared with her death? But Berger doesn't stay there. From the death of mothers, he shows us how, through the long, slow, sad pacing of centuries, mutations and selections, the brachiation of the arms of our animal ancestors are becoming, become ours.

8.

When I was deciding whether or not to try to become a mother, a friend began work on a collaborative play about women deciding not to have children and women unable to have children that they want.

Animal Animal Mammal Mine sets the relatively brief timespan of a woman's reproductive life within the long and sad timeline of evolution and the even longer and sadder history of the Earth: human fertility from the vantage of climate change and mass extinction.

In my friend's play, whimsy is never very far from the grotesque. Glaciers melt and toy helicopters hover over them. Women's bodies are policed, by the police, who wear the masks of ruminants.

It's also not really a play, maybe in the same way that these are not really essays, though the essay, as a genre, allows for its own unreliability. "I'm not a play-play kind of person," she told me once.

Bodies deliver dialogue and narrative, but they're also just bodies. Cast members grow wings, move gazelle-like through the shadows, and build nests (more rats' than birds') in the corners of the set. Increasingly unpredictable weather interrupts all other action as forms of painfully gradual dance.

I never saw my friend's play that wasn't really a play, at least not in real life, in the theater. I told her I couldn't help make a play about not becoming a mother because I was too busy trying to imagine whether or not to become a mother. And both sides of possibility frightened me.

Instead, I watched a recording on my laptop in an empty dorm room where I had travelled from California to upstate New York to teach students over the summer about language and thinking.

9.

My friend and I had worked together before. When we were students, we'd made a very short film based on the very long Japanese novel, *The Tale of Genji.*

When the novel was written, Japanese was largely a colloquial, and so a feminized language. The men at court wrote in Chinese for matters of both art and politics. So, one of the first novels in world literature was written by a woman, necessarily so.

I read only a selection, in a class, in translation. Being young myself, I was taken with Genji's self-imposed exile and papery loves.

The important thing about Genji's exile, which I learned from my teacher and not from my reading, is that he doesn't actually travel very far at all: roughly the distance from upper Manhattan to Brooklyn.

This maybe negligible distance was the subject of our film. No one knows the real name of *Genji*'s author. She is named for the lover he abandons when he goes into exile, Murasaki, which is also the Japanese word for a color, stranded on one end of the spectrum: purple lady, paper life.

When my friend visited me when I was first teaching in Japan, we made a pilgrimage to the place where *Genji* was written. There was an imaginary Murasaki, a life-sized doll holding a quill at a desk, purple kimono, white socks. We tried to film her with a camera we'd borrowed from the school, but the film was later damaged, or lost. And anyway, she wasn't moving so what was there to see.

Before that, we'd made another film together that also features purple. In it, I play a woman, probably a mother, who locks herself out of her car at a grocery store in rural Pennsylvania and pushes a large shopping cart piled with groceries, including a purple bag of cat food that matches her skirt, through the countryside to a development in what was recently a cornfield, where my character presumably lives. The last shot is of her pushing the cart in between these cookie-cutter houses and the black nets surrounding trampolines, early spring sky looming.

Along the way, she is transformed by the landscape through which she walks. She leaves behind the sprawl, the work park, and the highway median. She crosses a stone-bridge, takes off her heels, and makes friends with a horse.

In the first film, a man leaves a woman. In the second, a woman leaves a certain version of herself. No one now, including you, dear reader, will ever see these films, so you will have to imagine. I am a terrible actor. Imagine that too.

10.

Becoming a mother is becoming mingled. Some form kicks me in the side when I sit down to have a thought. Hiccups and limbs, anxieties and anticipation. If you live with a heart outside your body, your heart becomes an encountering thing. Gravity no longer a unifying universal force, menace, or wearying reminder: this body is not this body alone. I can't say what I need to say without this body wrestling this body in the direction of disembodied print.

This class begins: literature takes place in the present, even when what you are reading is medieval, or from a few years ago, or written this week. This is a convention students rarely question. Others they find less intuitive, like whether an "I" should be allowed in. An education has taught them to keep themselves out of an argument.

Sometimes you can't.

Sometimes the best thinking happens in the midst, or in the mist, where thoughts mingle with chrysanthemums, singed vegetal matter, or the vertigo of desecrated loves.

It may be that life within a perpetual present is damaged life, timeliness wrested from this and that.

At the end of class, I ask what "Possibility" might mean in Dickinson's poem, reminding them to set their readings in the present tense.

One of the students excuses his self. She, the poet, is imagining her house and the children she'll have and how she'll be happy.

I ask where he sees that in the poem. I let myself outside.

Since this is California, it's easy enough, doors open to the eucalyptus and the desiccating spring.

11.

I don't know much about the Romantics, but I do know that when Percy Bysshe Shelley and Mary Godwin started dating, they would sometimes meet by the grave of Mary's mother, Mary Wollstonecraft.

Wollstonecraft is the author of *A Vindication of the Rights of Woman*, which I was reading once when helping a lover canvas for a city council race. We—volunteers—were crammed into an elevator when one of my lover's friends started laughing at my book.

I remember thinking he was asking me a question and then realizing he wasn't interested at all, in anything I was reading or might have to say about it. Then we stood on the corner together and handed out leaflets.

It was an inconsequential race. Later, he became a lawyer, and defended prisoners on death row.

12.

Mary Wollstonecraft died giving birth to Mary Godwin, which is to say, she died a month after the supposed event of childbirth, which is to say, her death was caused by birth.

Mary Godwin later became Mary Shelley, and wrote *Frankenstein*, which we often think of as a book about a monster but is really a ghost story about the tragedy of human reproduction and the destruction of family feeling, which Mary Shelley wrote after the death of her first child and published after the deaths of her second and third.

Mary Wollstonecraft's first book was *Letters Written in Sweden, Norway, and Denmark*. The letters were to her lover, who was American, and missing. She was in Scandinavia pursuing his gold. She carried their daughter, little Fanny Imlay, with her in the coast-born boats. Years later, Fanny Imlay killed herself. All deaths are caused by births.

In his "Defence of Poetry," Mary Shelley's lover, a poet, describes the dispossessing turmoil of the imagination as pregnancy and birth: "a sympathy with pains and passions so mighty, that they distend in their conception the capacity of that by which they are conceived."

In her "Introduction" to the 1831 edition of *Frankenstein*, Mary Shelley describes the growth of her imagination as far from her self, mixed with trees and raging mountains.

Which is to say, there is a place for the illegitimate children of the imagination. "Conceived" is a word the poet uses, but she chooses another. These "airy flights," she writes, "fostered," loved, and free.

"I did not make myself the heroine of my tales," she writes. "Life appeared to me too commonplace an affair as regarded myself...and I could people the hours with creations far more interesting to me, at that age, than my own sensations."

"After this," she writes, "my life became busier," and, in consequence with that escalation and those stillbirths, "reality stood in the place of fiction."

Before I was a mother, I was sometimes a teacher. Once, when I taught *Frankenstein*, I could barely read it. Because I wanted so badly to become a mother that I couldn't handle the doctor's poor parenting of his monster? Because I was too distracted by life to devote the time it takes to live within a novel? Because I was still learning to become a teacher? Because my students, in their partially concealed lives, in the privacy of their reading, were my monsters?

One of them was pregnant, then. I couldn't imagine what she was thinking.

13.

Imagination and memory are structurally very similar, though one looks backwards, and one looks off into the future, into the glaring sun. Both have to do with the creation of worlds, selves, experiences that aren't immediately available. And the power of each has to do with the degree to which their retrospective or projective powers can make what is distant feel materially present.

Before I began becoming a mother, I lived for several years with a friend in a Victorian duplex on the side of a hill in San Francisco. When we lived there, the neighborhood was continuing to change, from mostly middle class to mostly very wealthy. In the 1950s, the neighborhood had been almost entirely working class, nicknamed "Red Hill" for the many dockworkers with communist leanings that lived there. In 2009, there was a small bookstore called "Red Hill Books," with a well-stocked Kids section. Most of our neighbors had kids. We were outliers, students riding our bikes up and down the hill. Our house was garishly white and red and almost neon blue. Now it is gray, and we live on opposite coasts.

We used to cook a lot together. I remember my friend shelling chestnuts late into the night in front of a laptop playing some 1930s screwball comedy until her hands broke out in a rash; then she candied the chestnuts and canned them. Another Saturday, our first together in the apartment, we came home from the farmers market and made a goat cheese and herby soufflé, for lunch, just for us and another friend. The giant billowy thing collapsed before we could eat hardly any of it. A soufflé is something you should make with broader company in mind.

Then she moved north up the coast to Oregon. I moved south along the coast in California, and then east to Massachusetts. Her child was born two years before mine. We still cook a lot, but rarely together. Now our friendship lives in emails and phone calls, the occasional exchange of unfinished essays or poems. Now that we have become mothers, we have become editors, too.

14.

One of my best friends growing up was a man but wasn't manifesting as one yet. As with other men I was embroiled with when I was younger, we used to argue. Once, as teenagers, we argued about whether, if a man could give birth, he "should."

I don't remember exactly where the "should" of this argument was grounded: in law, government, institutions, choice. Or who or what we each imagined was on the other side, regulating permission. At the time, it seemed obvious (only to me) that this was a matter of what was "natural." No, men shouldn't be mothers because that's not what mothers "are." What does it mean to "be" anything, my friend counteracted, and who gets to decide what is "nature"? I realize now how much these discussions tangled in different understandings of language's ability to make visible what would otherwise remain hidden. We used to argue about whether or not I should love women. That was an argument that, by example, I won. By that logic, my friend won this old argument, becoming a man who could become a mother. Though, now that he is a parent, he is "100% father," he clarifies by text.

15.

My child was alive for a long time before my son or daughter was alive, but I couldn't see. This child grabbed its ear or put her fingers in her mouth like this before he was born.

In one of our birth classes, the midwife describes the pain of childbirth as "transitional," like the pain of losing a tooth, or a child's body expanding in the night. I don't remember either of these pains, pain of being turned into a person out of what went before, pain of I becoming you. But I do know, even before becoming a mother, what Emerson called, even before the death of his son, the "pain of an alien world." That is the pain I fear most when I decide to become a mother.

In the months following my child's first birthday, as it/he/she begins to walk and point and nod and make sounds in the directions of ideas and things, I begin to imagine motherhood again. Up until now, becoming a mother has been too much an entirely physical thing; when mothering does lead into flights of fancy, they tend to be of the nightmarish kind: what if my grip slips, what if the stroller runs away into the road, what if the ocean suddenly rises up to swallow us here in the shallows whole?

But now I find, on the bike ride to daycare, that I am imagining names (the same thing that before becoming a mother, I found unimaginable). When a teacher says, this child has a good heart, this child is the kind of person the world needs more of, you should have another child, I am flattered enough for both of us to imagine it. When I tell my husband that night about our child's day with others, he tells me that he dreamed the night before we had a daughter. I was alone at the birth, he said.

How did that work? I ask. You were just somewhere else, he says. It was strange. That doesn't bode well, I say. No, nothing terrible, he affirms. It was a work thing. So I was off teaching somewhere, and not dying in childbirth, while our daughter was being born? Yes, something like that, he says. I didn't know where you were. It was a dream.

That night, I dream that one of my childhood friends who is now a teacher collapses in my arms as her water breaks, but it's me who is hunting for a taxi under some overpass in New York. The dream has become an all too familiar scene of television delivery. I need to get to the hospital *now*. This woman—but my friend is no longer beside me—is having a baby! But the baby isn't a part of the dream.

Later, when we talk on the phone about teaching, she tells me she's had a miscarriage. Another friend, about her miscarriage says, It—the thing—wasn't growing. I needed to get it out.

16.

After the birth of my child, I lie in bed for a long time reading. Partly because I want to know what other women have written about becoming mothers, and partly because I can barely walk. When I say a long time, what I mean is several weeks, and then for months afterwards. Also, my breasts or my vagina leak every time I go anywhere, which is embarrassing. I prefer to read and not to leak.

I read Alice Notley, and Rachel Zucker, and, along with much of a small section of the rest of the American reading public, Maggie Nelson's *The Argonauts*. If you find yourself in a similar situation, or if you want to know more about how poems can migrate into conversations (or arguments), or prose can swoop onward in conversation with itself, I can recommend these three writers to you. For each of them, motherhood, and writing, means something different; but for each, motherhood and writing are relational. I also read the second book of

Karl Ove Knausgaard's *My Struggle*. There is a fantastic scene in which his wife, who is also a writer, gives birth to their first child. She is given gas during labor, which is rarely used in the United States, and keeps saying, throughout labor, the gas is "fantastic." If you find yourself in a different situation, this might be a better book for you.

Sometime in the '90s, I read an article by Francine Prose that was about whether or not women writers necessarily wrote *as* women, whether women could ever escape their bodies enough to inhabit a language that was otherwise apart from them, genderless. I remember the thesis bothering me, like a bad itch I didn't yet know how to scratch.

After the 2016 election, Hilary Mantel wrote an essay that I read before falling asleep by myself. (My husband was sleeping on the love seat in our child's room.) It's an essay about choice, but before she explains this, the author recalls herself as a younger woman, once when she thought she was pregnant, before that thought, or hope, or whatever you might call it—she calls it "imagination"—was shredded by an encompassing pain.

But the imagination doesn't leave with the body, like a headache properly dosed. "Fragile, fallible," she writes, "it goes on working in the world."

The child she imagined may have been ectopically material or flighty as fancy, the faculty Coleridge saw as more earthly than the imagination, and so the lesser of the two. Fancy-work became women's work, at its most ornamental: lace or embroidery, never quite something one could entirely see through.

17.

When my child was becoming restless enough to prefer sprawling on the floor or pulling up on chairs, we ventured out in search of conversation. We met a friend in an art museum. She is a professor and not a mother. We talked about genre.

She said: we choose genres based on what we need to work on in life. If you study novels, you may have something to learn about character and plot, narrative and foreshadowing. If you study poetry, you may have trouble with form.

That essay by Lukács about Kierkegaard, the one that is not about "die werkliche Frau," but that nevertheless also is, is called "The Foundering of Form Against Life." Later, Lukács became one of the foremost theorists of realist fiction.

If I have trouble with form, I have realism, however, to blame. Not that this character looks or speaks as she does in real life. I learned from her indirectly, while watching my child pull and reach. A poem, inculcation within absence, not structure itself.

The art museum, mostly windows, interrupting us with light.

18.

One more mother appears in Berger's essay, two short paragraphs after his mother dies.

But it is not Berger's mother: "It is thanks to hanging from trees that one of the actors can throw himself into the arms of a mother and cry," Berger writes. "Brachiation gave us breasts to beat and to be held against. No other animal can do these things."

Berger's essay is about, as much as an essay like this is ever truly about any one thing, watching animals as if watching theater. The actor with arms and breasts is an ape. But she is also his mother. He imagines mothering even after his mother has gone. In another book, he imagines meeting his mother again and again, in an alleyway in Portugal, balanced along a precarious roof. There, she appears and disappears as if from nowhere, though always mid-conversation. There should be a literary term for this. Like *media res,* or *ex machina*, but without ever being really before or after, memory or imagination, and without a god.

19.

I wrote this poem some time ago and then decided, when writing this, that it was no longer a poem.

My mother says she wants to see the Northern Lights, it begins. I'm deciding not to label bottles in a pantry, it continues, allowing for disarray. I turn my mother like turning a corner.

One night we are driving home, the Hudson Valley turns on like noon. It's only later we learn: meteor. But then we imagine something more world historical, a new world, this blue otherwise hidden in the blank of night.

My mother likes to look at movement in the sky. Never saw herself from outside as someone preoccupied with nature. That was her mother, the one that stopped cars at roadsides to cradle wildflowers in her hands. My mother steals lilies and ferns from roadsides and buries them in her garden. She pulls rosemary from the bush. She observes rain falling on Vermont as streaky gray disturbance. She pulls us out of bed to see the moon eclipsing above the orchard. She asks to stop the bus in the middle of the desert for the sake of the stars.

She wants to see the Northern Lights before she dies, says my mother, who was wounded when her mother was dying and didn't say, who says, when she has to say something, when I say I wish we spoke more easily and often, she hopes my life will be filled with all the joys she's known.

POPPY/
FRIEND

with Juliana Chow

Letter 1 (November 14, 2012)

Dear Jules,

Let's begin with poppies.

Eschscholzia californica is not a true poppy, though it shares with Ranunculales a frilly, parsley-like leafage, and with Papaveraceae an apparent fragility and love of roadsides.

Its genus is named for one German naturalist, Johann Friedrich von Eschscholtz, by another, Adelbert von Chamisso. These two flower-friends traveled together to California, among other exotic locals, from Russia, sometime during 1815–1818, and published their results in 1822.

In California, as we both know, our poppy is prolific. It will grow through pavement, or around the feet of grazing cattle. Its shape is more triangular than those species with which it shares a common name. It twists shut at night, curling around itself into a beak-like cone. And it sits on a small reddish saucer, which is as stiff and circular as its petal ends are ragged and pliable. At its center, a small tuft of orange or yellow reproductive fluff. And it is itself yellow or orange, rarely white, or some gradation of these.

It is not a plant native to New England. And yet, we know that it was cultivated there with some regularity in the nineteenth century. By the 1830s, *Eschscholzia californica* is presented in New England periodicals as a common, though somewhat troublesome, cultivated plant. The plant appears under the heading "New Plants" in the May 18, 1833 issue of *The Genesee Farmer and Gardener's Journal* and makes entries into three editions of the *Horticultural Register and Gardener's Magazine* during 1835 and 1836.

In Emily Dickinson's herbarium, assembled in the 1840s, our poppy appears at the bottom middle of a page including seven other specimens, two without names. The other plants are nodding trillium; a purplish common garden tulip; starflower; a downy false foxglove— which Dickinson mislabels *Aureolaria pedicularia*, common name fern-leaved foxglove—and fern-leaved foxglove—which Dickinson mislabels *Aureolaria flava*, common name smooth false foxglove. Between these two erroneous foxgloves: our California poppy, whose four yellow petals are wrinkled like unsmoothed cotton, the top two dog-eared over on the center like pages of a tiny, unreadable book.

In the descriptions of *Eschscholzia* in New England in the nineteenth century, the plant is prized both for its ornamental showiness, and its invocation of an otherwise inaccessible, sunnier clime. "Scarcely any plant produces a greater degree of splendor than this," one author writes in 1836; "when the full sun is upon it, it makes a complete blaze of color. It is the most suitable plant for producing a distant effect." One of Emily Dickinson's textbooks while she was at Mount Holyoke, Alphonso Wood's *A Class Book of Botany*, describes *Eschscholzia* as "A very showy annual, common in our gardens."

For a few decades, then, the California poppy serves an additive function in New England gardens: an approximation of a wild within an increasingly tame space. By the second half of the century, however,

Eschscholzia ceases to appear primarily as a garden plant; indeed, it disappears from eastern periodicals almost entirely. The inclusion of an "Embroidery Design" based on the poppy's frills, triangles, and flame-like colors, ideal for "the end of a bureau scarf" in the New York based *Harper's Bazaar* in 1894 signals the plant's increasingly ornamental nature in the east.

Recently, Theo Davis has described an ornamental aesthetics in nineteenth-century literature that attends to the artifice of beauty as it *animates* attention. This animation moves beyond a singular attentiveness to accurately describe the presence of the California poppy in New England nineteenth-century gardens, where it projects the wild rather than being synonymous with wildness, making history happen—giving Emily Dickinson a page of flowers to press, and later, lady-readers of *Harper's* a design to embroider at the end of a scarf. Later still, the poppy becomes an emblem for the state from which it hails: our flower. All of this contributes to an aesthetic based on the surprising agency of a plant.

Davis develops her notion of ornamental aesthetics from, among other examples, the lilies Henry David Thoreau describes during his river-paddle in *A Week on the Concord and Merrimack Rivers*. Thoreau looks at these flowers, but they also elude him, as does the ornamental itself, always glinting and growing. Davis describes this encounter as an "adjacency" that "does not reach communication or even recognition."

That not quite communicative adjacency is evocative, also, of letter writing, and of friendship. The letter is a sub-literary, supplemental genre. Its intimacies are indirect. Sometimes its vectors run straight through their mark and are more beautiful than the bullseye and so detract from intention or attachment. An ornamental affection: attachment in motion.

Letter 2 (January 17–23, 2013)

Dear Gillian,

I have often wondered if you had you not been at Berkeley the same year and in the same discipline, would I now be lost in a different period and nation other than nineteenth-century America? Because you loved Dickinson, I began to read and love her, too. Because you loved Melville and Emerson, I read them, too, and though I could not love them they had for me a luster that comes from well-worn appraisal.

Sometimes it seems to me that we took each other's half-formed thoughts, a suggestive scent and warmth, the way flipping through pages of a recipe book gives rise to swells and pangs, and said them back to each other as though hearing them in another's voice would give them air. We need only say "bewilderment" and each of us is on a wild chase in dark woods. "Bewilderment." "Poppy." "Chrysoprase." "Ornamental." Epiphytes fed on each other's breath. I know we are in our own wildernesses with its own echoes—and I have always thought of myself as more an echo: "what's mine is yours"—but perhaps I do not know myself.

That I gave you seeds from California poppies growing against the edges of sidewalks of 43rd Street in Oakland, that you noticed the poppy in Emily Dickinson's herbarium, on the bottom of page 43 between two false foxgloves, that Celia Thaxter wrote so reverently of the poppy and cultivated it in her garden on Appledore Island off the New England coast, that you came here, that I grew up here, that we met here.

As you mentioned, the California poppy, *Eschscholzia californica*, was named in amity by Chamisso for Eschscholtz during a voyage which toured the Pacific coast ostensibly in search of a northwest passage. The Russian expedition of the *Rurik* set out in the summer of 1815, rounding Cape Horn on January 22, 1816 and passing through Kamchatka in July on the way to Alaska. It began its southward voyage in the fall, and from October 1 to November 1, the *Rurik* anchored in the San Francisco Bay before plunging west to explore the islands of the Pacific. Chamisso and Eschscholtz spent most of their time in California collecting in and around the Presidio and the Mission:

> The fogs, which the prevailing sea-winds blow over the coast, dissolve in summer over a heated and parched soil, and the country exhibits in autumn only the prospect of bare scorched tracts, alternating with poor stunted bushes, and in places, with dazzling wastes of drift sand. Dark pine forests appear here and there on the ridge of the mountains, between the Punta de los Reyes and the harbour of San Francisco. The prickly-leaved oak, *Quercus agrifolia*, is the most common and largest tree. With crooked boughs and entangled branches, it lies, like the other bushes, bent towards the land; and the flattened tops, swept by the sea-wind, seem to have been clipped by the gardener's shears. The Flora of this country is poor, and is not adorned by one of those species of plants which are produced by a warmer sun...

The season was not very favourable for us. We, however, gathered the seeds of several plants, and have reason to hope that we shall be able to enrich our gardens with them.

I recognize, as you do, Chamisso's description of San Francisco: the fog that rolls in thick and cold over the peninsula, the perpetual drought that burnishes the hills with yellow grasses, relieved only by winter rains which these days seem ever scarcer. It is windswept and parched, poor and novel, unfavorable and enriching.

I wish that there might have been more to say of the San Francisco we shared; there is a limit to the imagination that I circumnavigate here. Perhaps we were defeated by that interminable distance between the "there" and "no there there" that separates San Francisco from Oakland, more easily acquiesced to than plumbed for depths. And yet the few times I came over—berrying at Bernal Hill, a walk through Glen Canyon, visits to your apartment—these were like explorations of Joseph Cornell's curiosity cabinets except that they were yours not mine.

I remember looking out the window of your living room at dusk, seeing the cascade of lights on Portola Hill gradually appear, and feeling uneasy but also deeply compelled by the ornate quiet. You had made tea and cut a slice of homemade brioche spread with jam, laid this all out on a tea table for me. Later, the chilly night enveloped me as I walked down to Glen Park to catch the train home. All the way back I carried with me the sense that we were playing house, that we were kindergarteners still learning the letters of the alphabet and how to sing songs.

I cannot tell if it is only me that pretends to be there, if you are pretending with me, or if I am missing out on certain intricacies of a game. Across from me you spell out a string of words I don't know how to read yet, and like someone translating a speech into sign language, you mouth the words and make concise gestures. It is magical.

Emerson: "but it is necessary to write a letter to a friend."

What is a friendship written in letters? What more could it be other than letters? A's, and b's, and c's, and d's.

Emerson characterizes the highest friendship as "an absolute running of two souls into one." This is the rarefied meeting of two shining forms—the "evanescent intercourse" of star-crossed figures, a "spiritual astronomy" of greatness beckoning greatness and pure molten transference. A lit oil slick melds with liquid fire but shuns the watery spread of those beneath. "Let him be to me a spirit," he wrote, "A message, a thought, a sincerity, a glance from him, I want, but not news, nor pottage…Let him be to thee for ever a sort of beautiful enemy, untamable, devoutly revered."

But what is the difference really between the jealous spite of Emerson's "Thine ever, or never" and his cool proclamation that "the not mine is mine," when both are still conceived in mine and thine?

Of his time botanizing on the *Rurik* expedition, Chamisso wrote, "I always studied, observed, and collected together with my faithful Eschscholtz. In complete harmony, we never distinguished between mine and thine."

June 9–July 6, 1820

Dear Adelbert,

Your scientific botanical discourses anew wandered through my almost sleeping passion for botany.

In St. Laurence Bay where Ranunculus chamissonis grew (and where we quarrelled!!) is a variety of Dispersia with pinkish-red flowers that remarkably no one has mentioned yet. Do you remember such in a dried state? If not, at the next opportunity I will send it to you…I'm pleased with the possibility of increasing the family of Hippuris with a new species; did you really never see the bedstraw near a little sedge which we found very high up in the mountains in Unalaska in wet places? It is a miniature plant, rolled up in its leaves. Now, check! That method of botanizing has already furnished me with three plants, namely, besides that one, another large-sized bedstraw in Unalaska and the little pennywort with linear leaves; I can't remember if it was from Brazil or from Chile. This Hippuris (it needs to be called montana) is two and a half to three inches in size with whorls of leaves, placed far apart, usually with six or eight leaflets, the leaflets linear, acute…One specimen is enclosed in this letter; report only if you found it among your sedges, then I will send you good specimens.

Now I want to bring up something else: in this letter I often gave the names of new species; do not consider this as a presumption but only as a suggestion. Of course, you are free to preserve or reject them. I certainly would not want the name which is put in place of my name to be only "N."

Now, farewell, dear companion of my military cruise! Aroha!

Your Abigar

N.B. I still haven't received from the bookstore the dissertation you sent!

According to their arrangement apparently agreed upon in their early days on board the *Rurik*, Chamisso would describe the plants and Eschscholtz the insects. After they parted ways, their work together continued in correspondence. While Chamisso's letters to Eschscholtz have been lost, Eschscholtz's to him were found in the collections of the Berlin State Library, perhaps left there somehow among Chamisso's papers.

Following Tahitian custom, Eschscholtz had exchanged names with "Abigar" and Chamisso with "Rarik," inhabitants of coral islands they later visited. This naming was apparently a kind of bond made between two friends—one described by James Morrison in a 1935 description as a wedding between two friends, often men, rather than a bride and groom. Called a *taio* friendship by eighteenth and nineteenth-century European voyageurs who were greeted by Polynesians with this term, and variously transliterated also as *tayo*, *tio*, *tyo*, and *taillot*, the bond stipulated the free exchange of gifts between such friends. Some common items the Europeans traded were metal tools and other goods rare in the islands, as well as what they considered "trifles" or "gifts" depending on their magnanimity, while the Polynesians offered food, drink, clothes, and even sex. As the name exchange indicates, the *taio* was an alliance between two specific individuals—Eschscholtz's with Abigar and Chamisso's with Rarik—that subsequently seemed to bring the individuals together into a coupling, a wedding, in which the boundaries of mine and thine dissolved.

Emerson notes the exchange of not only letters but also names in his essay on friendship as well: "Men have sometimes exchanged names with their friends, as if they would signify that in their friend each loved his own soul." His transcendentalist version, however, deliberately elides cultural and linguistic differences, and indeed the entire context of the Polynesian islands.

As early nineteenth-century European travelers to the Pacific islands where imperialism converged with scientific exploration, what alliance, what friendship, could Chamisso and Eschscholtz have had with the island people? Chamisso later published the first book to technically describe Hawaiian language in 1837, drawing upon the dictionaries of European missionaries to the Pacific islands. What can we make of the momentary tropical climate generated by their fond quips to each other as "Your Abigar" and "Your Rarik"? Aroha! Vanessa Smith writes of *taio* as emerging out of "a complex compound of economics and affect, never fully reducible to one or the other," to become cross-cultural friendships that are "neither the pure products of the global relations that enable them nor of the emotional responses they engender." Strangely, the word *taio* is no longer used in contemporary Tahitian lexicon, its existence only confirmed by European accounts of their encounters with natives. Smith again: "They announce absences rather than achieved presences in the historical record."

They had their quarrels, their parenthetical breaks and moody furloughs. Eschscholtz's "surprise" that Chamisso did not observe a particular flower precedes a similar moment in California, where they sailed next. Chamisso relates this event in his *Journal*:

> In a swamp, near by our tent, a water-plant had [is supposed to have] grown, which Eschscholtz asked me about after our departure. I had not observed it; he, however, had reckoned that a water-plant, my especial love, would not have escaped me, and did not wish to get his feet wet. So much may one expect by relying on one's friends!

If Unalaska was where they had quarreled, it was also where they decided to *not* study, observe, and collect together. Chamisso notes on this leg of their journey: "Eschscholtz was gathering plants on his own. We had found out that it was better for us to separate on land, as we had enough of each other on board ship." Whatever had come between the two, it meant that Eschscholtz went botanizing in the mountains on his own and did not return after nightfall. *Rurik* captain Kotzebue appointed Chamisso in charge of a search and they combed the mountains, returning to find Eschscholtz already back on the ship, having made his way down in the morning. In his recollections of this event, Chamisso is more concerned about his own safety and miffed at not being recognized for the danger he encountered when leading the search party. Of Eschscholtz he says little.

"Before the flowers of friendship faded friendship faded": Stein.

Perusing Chamisso's *Notes and Remarks*, his *Journal*, and Eschscholtz's letters to Chamisso, it is as though I come upon the dry dead land that greeted them in California, too late for the spring flowering season, too late for friendships, left only with these letters:

> Hence, it must be acknowledged that I am tireless in correspondence. This is already the fourth letter I've sent after your latest. I assume, however, that several of my letters, and also maybe one of yours, have been lost.

Emerson wrote, "To my friend I write a letter, and from him I receive a letter. That seems to you a little. It suffices me." And yet in the letters of Eschscholtz to Chamisso, letter-writing is not an occasional brilliant transfusion, but a kind of desperate efflorescence, respiring and expiring extravagantly. The many letters written and mulled over, entrusted to various couriers—one of whom died enroute—lost or delayed by the contingencies of transportation, national postal services, and the demands of daily life—lectures to read, collections to preserve and maintain, families, students, scholarly societies—and still they wrote.

Imagine also the collections and packets of seeds and dried plants circulating to and fro, around the Americas to Europe and elsewhere as collectors and botanists sent—and lost—specimens to each other throughout the eighteenth and nineteenth centuries, of which the flower and scientific notes in Eschscholtz's letter are only one small mote.

Emerson again: "Only the star dazzles; the planet has a faint, moonlike ray." Nietzsche, from "Star Friendship":

> We were friends, and have become strangers to each other. But perhaps this is as it ought to be—and we do not want either to

conceal or obscure the fact as if we had to be ashamed. We are two ships each of which has its own goal and course. Our paths may cross and we may celebrate a feast together, as we did—and then the good ships rested so quietly in one harbor and in one sunshine that it may have looked as if they had reached their goal and as if they had but one goal. But then the almighty force of our tasks drove us apart again into different seas and sunny zones…There is probably a tremendous but invisible stellar orbit in which our very different ways and goals may be included as small parts of this path— let us rise up to this thought. But our life is too short and the power of our vision too limited for us to be more than friends in the sense of this sublime possibility. Let us then believe in our stellar friendship, though we should have to be terrestrial enemies to one another.

And so our Earth is only an echo of the sun's radiance, and the further we go from the equatorial latitudes the farther we are from those sunny harbors: "The Flora of this country is poor, and is not adorned by one of those species of plants which are produced by a warmer sun." In this dry and hot winter of California, I write to you. Am I one of your friends? How could I be? It is almost as though one really must be on board the same ship for three years together, in such cramped quarters and sharing the same rote household joys. We must live together to that appalling degree of petty quarrels and pet names and open secrets—I disagree with Emerson's discounting of these pastimes—to reach the familiarity that erodes glossy sublimation. So we have failed, perhaps from lack of wanting, or from those very obstacles that accompany all letter-writing and sending.

And yet we still do these things for each other—send letters, attend weddings, meet for lunches and walks—driven by some sense of fortuity and vague amity. I cannot tell who was bewildered first, which flower drew whose attention, what words haunt whom more. This is a letter sent to you for someone else, for many others else. We write letters not for each other but for the culmination of their post-hour. To see them flare up and expire like fireworks or shooting stars, petals shed and pressed. They lose their brilliance so fast, must be collected and renewed annually.

The California poppy grown away from its drift lands is "unsatisfactory." The letters written and received are "unsatisfactory." "Lord, when shall we ever stop growing?" A poppy friendship is unassuming, almost careless in its attachments. We are swept up in the general calamity of things, directionless or in-all-directions, dispersing flowers, messages, a glance, and a poem, profusely and generously without regard for their deliverance. There is a lithe, skirting pattern one could draw from the scatter of our thoughts and affections, a sketch of the routes we make from coast to coast, peninsula to insular bay, sometimes meeting, sometimes not. We are friends, we are close to friends, we are nearly friends, we are—how do you spell that?—

Letter 3 (April 1–30, 2013)

Dear Jules,

I often wonder how many times Hawthorne read Melville's letters (that we have read so recursively for over a century). Did he jam them into a drawer and draw back his hand from the shock? Or did he sit around in the evening by the fire, Sophia painting, or reading, turning their pages over one another, savoring. I think of all genres, the epistle's dis-honesties are the most upsetting. It's all very well for an outsider, a hundred years in the distance, but how terrible for the persons caught in these convoluted discretions. Some letters feel like pins in pretty dresses, mocked up for an unrealized body; whether the pins are there for pricking or for keeping the folded cambric in place, what does the body know? Generally, when I am the body I don't read well, wincing and dancing too much to keep still. This restlessness feels appropriate to poppies. It is spring now, and I have been amiss and inattentive. It has taken me months to respond. The green of California's winter hills is drying away into barren gold again. And orange transfusions have returned to the slopes.

In her first letter to Abiah Root, the late girlhood friend toward whom Dickinson would compose twenty-two letters between 1845 and 1854, Dickinson brags about her plants and refers to the incomplete nature of a shared education. "My plants look beautifully." "Old King Frost has not had the pleasure of snatching any of them in his cold embrace as yet, and I hope will not." Later in the letter she writes: "We'll fin-ish an education sometime, won't we?" February 23, 1845. What plants was Dickinson preserving from the frost? What were these two girls learning?

I have an image of you from our first year in school together. Standing among the fruit at the Berkeley Bowl, taking a piece and smelling it, touching it, how deliberately you moved through the aisles and how I had to swallow half of every step in order to keep pace. The fruit is un-clear. Your fingers and face compose much of the frame. We had plans to make dinner. And afterwards we sat at that black table in the rough center of my mostly empty studio apartment and talked. Deliberately, too, I imagine. The details are occluded, but I remember the rhythm of our exchanges because they unfurled differently from my everyday patterns and surges. I bluster, Jules, when you linger. I shatter Sevres (recalling another of Dickinson's poems, about sharing a life). And perhaps, for that reason, a tea tray has begun to seem to me like a stay against chaos and death, much as Robert Frost thought a poem was. An evidently elaborate notion. A sentence pulled from Woolf. When I read Rhoda or Lily Briscoe, I remember you. But perhaps friends should not remember one another, or find one another in works of art. "Dear Remembered," Dickinson addresses Abiah in May of 1850 after their intimacy has slowed. Perhaps friends should not write letters at all.

Dickinson speaks of her flowers as friends, and of her friends as flowers. Writing to Abiah, among other things, of the death of her friend Sophia Holland: "She was too lovely for the earth & she was transplanted from heaven to earth." Sophia's death is figured in flower terms, death as the gardener and loveliness the boon. Of this friendship, one half of its roots fast in heavenly soil, Dickinson writes: "I have never lost but one friend near my age & with whom my thoughts & her own were the same." Sophia was one flower and Abiah, now, another. "It was before you came to Amherst," Dickinson reassures her young friend, Root. May their thoughts be ever the same and the gardener and frost aloof.

Flowers are friends Dickinson can directly tend, misting and tucking, bearing away yellow leaves, coaxing perfumes. Frequently, she tells Abiah of the health of her charges and asks after the being and well-being of Abiah's own flower friends. In August 1845, Dickinson reports with pride: "My House plants look very finely now." A month later, "Have you any flowers now?" "I have had a beautiful flower-garden this summer; but they are nearly gone now."

The recurrence of now, now, now, echoes through the distance of epistles. When is the now that flowers are, that letters leave behind? In September of the next year, she asks Abiah, "Have you any flowers in Norwich?" And crows, "My garden looked finely when I left home."

This efflorescent context is the foundation of their friendship, at least so far as Dickinson is concerned. She affiliates Abiah with the flowers after whose bright presences she inquires. In an early letter, from January 1846, she writes, "I can hardly wait for spring to come, for I so long to see you," as if the very shift in season would usher along her friend, pulling crocuses from the bulb along with Abiah. In her penultimate letter to her friend in May 1852, Dickinson declares a long association: "Oh, Abiah, you and the early flowers are forever linked to me; as soon as the first green grass comes, up from a chink in the stones peeps the little flower, precious 'leontodon,' and my heart fills toward you with a warm and childlike fullness! Nor do I laugh now; far from it, I rather bless the flower which sweetly, slyly too, makes me come nearer you." Dickinson and Abiah had not met for years; their correspondence has had room for entire years of quiet and apart. Dickinson approaches her friend through the little dandelion along the garden walk. She does not leave her father's house. The flowers are all the more real and personable to her.

In November 1851, Melville asks his friend, his "fellow human," "Whence come you, Hawthorne? By what right do you drink from my flagon of life?" In May 1850, Dickinson asks, "Where are you now Abiah, where are your thoughts, and aspirings, where are your young affections?" Melville and Hawthorne have become tangled: "And when I put it to my lips," one writes, "lo, they are yours & not mine." It is the only letter written to Hawthorne that Melville signs, simply, Herman. It is one of the last. In Dickinson's letter to Abiah, two thirds of the way into their correspondence and after a major turning point in which Dickinson seems sure of the end of the friendship, she asks for remembrance, and for flowers: "Remember, and care for me sometimes, and scatter a fragrant flower in this wilderness life of mine by writing me, and by not forgetting." Forget-me-not was one of the flowers Dickinson earlier offered to send: tiny blue things with black and orange eyes. "Have you got any Forget me not in your garden this summer," she inquired five years earlier. "I am going to send you as a present in my letter next time. I am pressing some for all the girls and it is not dry yet." By 1850, Dickinson's herbarium is finished. Her garden is, doubtless, still in well health. But her mother is ailing, and her formal education is finished, and her wilderness requires words to wound it and keep it sufficiently stoked.

Melville performs in his letters to Hawthorne. Dickinson performs in her letters, too, teasing and fierce by turns. These are flashy documents. They stand on the edge of literary history and glitter and blink. But Dickinson's letters to Abiah are less ornamental; she is still working out the role of imagination when it comes to friends. In August 1845, she writes, "I have now sit down to write you a long, long letter. My writing apparatus is upon a stand before me, and all things are ready. I have no flowers before me as you had to inspire you. But then you know I can imagine myself inspired by them and perhaps that will do as well. You cannot imagine how delighted I was to receive your letter." The real flowers that accompany Abiah as she writes—or so Dickinson imagines—are replaced by imaginary ones. And Abiah "cannot imagine" Dickinson's delight in the letter that arrived from this friend. "I can imagine just how you look now," Dickinson writes. These declarations of a powerful imagination are offered as terms of endearment, but they also draw a wedge between this budding poetess and her flowery friend.

In these effusive early letters, Dickinson's assertions of her imaginary powers feel playful, like winking slights of hand. But by October 1848, something has damaged this friendly ease. "My own Abiah," this October letter begins before its author sets to fretting: "For so I will still call you, though while I do it, even now I tremble at my strange audacity, and almost wish I had been a little more humble not quite so presuming." Dickinson recounts a dream in which she searches for her friend in a crowd. "Slowly, very slowly," she writes, "I came to the conclusion that you had forgotten me, & I tried hard to forget you, but your image still haunts me, and tantalizes me with fond recollections." Their friendship has begun to turn on memory rather than imagination, and so the danger of being forgotten, or the necessity of forgetting, a willful erasure that the positive nature of imagination endlessly fills in, arrives: "if you dont want to be my friend any longer," Dickinson writes, "say so, & I'll try *once* more to blot you from my memory." The now, now, now of first letters resolves into a then.

In the next letter to Abiah—two years later!—Dickinson writes while under the influence of a fever. The document is wild and fictionally drenched. She talks of taking a stroll with "a little creature" who rides and wearies her, an illness come all the way from Switzerland. But the little monster, unlike Abiah, is demonstrative; it kisses her "immoderately, and express[es] so much love, it completely bewildered me." It lives with her and in the town. The letter is plumped with literary reference—*Macbeth*, Gray's "Elegy in a Country Churchyard," and Dickens's Christmas book of 1848, *The Haunted Man and the Ghost's Bargain*. The letter's author flexes: not so much a friend here, but a voice that can deflect far beyond the bounds of bodies or actual loves.

"Now my dear friend," she writes, "let me tell you that these last thoughts are fictions—vain imaginations to lead astray foolish young women. They are flowers of speech, they both *make* and *tell* deliberate falsehoods, avoid them as the snake, and turn aside as from the *Bottle* snake, and I don't *think* you will be harmed." Neither Dickinson's warnings nor her affections seem fully sincere. Perhaps it is the fever talking, or perhaps exaggeration itself has grown seductive:

> Wont you read some work upon snakes—I have a real anxiety for you! *I* love those little green ones that slide around by your shoes in the grass—and make it rustle with their elbows—they are rather my favorites on the whole, but I would'nt influence *you* for the world! There is an air of misanthropy about the striped snake that will commend itself at once to your taste…Something besides severe colds, and serpents, and we will try to find *that* something. It cant be a garden, can it, can it, or a strawberry bed, which rather belongs to a garden—nor it cant be a school-house, nor an Attorney at Law. Oh dear I don't know *what* it is! Love for the absent don't *sound* like it, but try it, and see how it goes.

I miss you very much indeed, think of you at night when the world's nodding, 'nidnid nodding[']—think of you in the daytime when the cares of the world, and it's toils, and it's continual vexations choke up the love for friends in some of our hearts; remember your warnings sometimes—try to do as you told me sometimes—and sometimes conclude it's no use to try; then my heart says it *is*, and new trial is followed by disappointment again. I wondered when you had gone why we didn't talk more…You astounded me in the outset—perplexed me in the continuance—and wound up in a grand snarl—I shall be all my pilgrimage unravelling.

What are we to make of this shift in tone? Dickinson writes to Abiah six more times across the course of four more years. References to rupture, demands for remembrance subside. After Abiah's marriage, they write no more. Is Dickinson fighting heartbreak with splendor? The fact of being forgotten by an amplification of indirection? She signs this letter, "Your very sincere, and *wicked* friend."

Letter 4 (June 27–30, 2014)

Dear Gillian,

I am back in California where it is hot, dry, and just a tad chilly when the wind blows. We spent the last days in Montreal and back to New Hampshire slogging through a warm summer rainstorm. Last summer there, we found black trumpets all along a back trail behind a ski mountain that had probably flooded with the rains and then receded, oysters sprouting from trees stumps in front yards, and chicken-of-the-woods.

No mushrooms here, and we have given up our arugula to turn into dry chaff.

For nineteenth-century New England gardeners to grow a poppy suited to dry, hot weather is a miracle; and yet they did. Perhaps Dickinson grew them, or a neighbor somewhere in Amherst. Celia Thaxter, another New England poet, grew them on Appledore Island of the Isles of Shoals off the coasts of New Hampshire and Maine. "Dear Feroline Fox," she writes on June 16, 1874, "My little garden sprang into such life of a sudden; all the seeds I planted, and a million more beside, came rushing up out of the ground so fast that I hardly knew how to manage them, and have been obliged to throw away enough flowers to stock half a dozen gardens, in order to let the remaining plants have room to grow. Such mats of pansies! And that flaming California poppy has spread everywhere. It breaks my heart to have to pull up a single one! Ranks of sweet-peas I have, and mignonette by the bushel. If I can only keep the weeds away!"

Thaxter decorated her father's hotel salon with the poppy's golden flares and the blooms of all the other rampaging plants from her garden. In a little guidebook on the isles, first published in 1873, John Scribner Jenness points to climate as the reason for its popularity as a summer resort, noting that "during the period from 1831 to 1843, it turns out, that while there are during the year, on the average, fifty-eight rainy days at Portland, and nearly fifty-eight at Boston, there are but twenty-five at the Piscataqua," by which he means the Portsmouth harbor area out of which one would sail for the isles. Though it may have been occasional and brief, a spell of dry weather in the middle of June, along with the rocky and barren grounds of the island, may have been just enough to coax profusions of California poppies far from home.

If this poppy was on its way to becoming a domesticated ornament of New England, it still retains for Thaxter something of wildness—and weediness. Its "spread everywhere," its bright orange petals warning of fire season in California, is in her New England garden similarly untamable. Along with "the million more beside," Thaxter's flowers are growing as wildly as the weeds she wants to keep away.

I have made a clearing here, sitting in a chair next to the door that opens out to the afternoon sunlight. It would be too easy to conclude that an enclosure such as this makes room for a letter to be written. In her 1894 *Island Garden*, Thaxter advises "of Poppies, Plant them in a rich sandy loam, all except the Californias (*Eschscholzia*), which do best in a poor soil." Pages later, of all the flowers she names, the California poppy is the one which Thaxter takes up as a prismatic emblem of the isles:

> As I hold the flower in my hand and think of trying to describe it, I realize how poor a creature I am, how impotent are words in the presence of such perfection. It is held upright upon a straight and polished stem, its petals curving upward and outward into the cup of light, pure gold with lustrous satin sheen; a rich orange is painted on the gold, drawn in infinitely fine lines to a point in the centre of the edge of each petal, so that the effect is that of a diamond of flame in a cup of gold.

Like her friend "Feroline Fox," whose alliterative name has a pixie ring to it, the flower is a fairy presence. Its elegance, however delicate, is too fine and too bejeweled in her description. Yet it is true that this diamond flame more brilliantly captures the California poppy than any other shade of orange, and if one must churn out words like cups of gold, it is better to be precise and piquant than staid and undistinguished.

When we visited you in Santa Barbara in May, you said you learned discipline from training in gymnastics, and it is with that same discipline you now approach your writing. But this discipline—and we all have our own versions of it; mine is to wake up by seven every morning, walk the dog, breakfast, and write until lunchtime, no more—is like turning dirt without fertilizer—"feeding / A little life with dried tubers." So far I have been lucky. The arugula and collards we planted last year sprang up again on their own after a thicket of spring rains in April. Perhaps the ones we leave to run to seed this year will turn the trick again. But somehow, I am less sure of it now that it isn't a surprise. The bloom has worn off. Writing feels the same once one must write the same thing over and over again as one does for a dissertation.

I thought moving to Santa Barbara sounded like a lovely writing retreat, and your new home seemed a quaint treehouse filled with old enamel kitchenware, tea trays with floral patterns, and the leafy arms of your rubber plant and fiddleleaf fig. It reminded me of Pablo Neruda's house in Santiago de Chile—all these little rooms winding around tree trunks, and every part of the house like a well-turned piece of driftwood strung with whimsical mobiles. But how can we write if all our will must go toward sweeping the floors and washing the dishes, and making a home of the place where we have come to? How can we write, even with all the discipline mustered, if the verdant enchantment of our lives is so much work to sustain? One could say the same thing of these texts that we turn over in our hands—there is a kind of dry academic paraphernalia of citations and critical trends that surround every word. Dutiful housekeeping of these hairy beasts that merely shed more every day—new facts, connections, and interpretations.

Something makes me want to throw it all away—though I fear that any new direction would yield the same vanity. I need little for inspiration—sometimes just a glass of water, a pencil, and paper—anything more would be distraction. Other times, it feels as though everything has gone dry, and even the novels I read to lead me astray are filled with familiar detours. When Charles Darwin marvels at how "the greatest amount of life diversity can be supported by great diversification of structure," he cites the example that "[i]t has been experimentally proved, that if a plot of ground be sown with one species of grass, and a similar plot be sown with several distinct genera of grasses, a greater number of plants and a greater weight of dry herbage can thus be raised." If we were to simply throw a greater diversity of things into our little plot of land, I suppose I am not sure if "a greater weight of dry herbage" is exactly the result I want. If we took Celia Thaxter's garden and pressed all the different species of flowers in an herbarium, she wouldn't have that certain heft of light that we know Dickinson by. But then, it is possible that neither would Dickinson. And what we are on the lookout for are these moments when a spark catches and burns, dangerously, vertiginously with wild growth.

What am I coaxing out of this letter? To Mrs. Horatio Lamb on March 13, 1893, Thaxter wrote:

> I send you one of Farquhar's catalogues, marked, as I promised,
> & I want to say about the marks, that they stand against flowers
> that I know about, intimately, & the more marks you find the

more charming & desirable is the flower! I dare say you know about them all, & I know there are many that are as beautiful, perhaps, which I have not marked, but these I have indicated are all old friends & dear, & I am sure of them. I am sure you'll have tulips & peonies, (don't forget the <u>single</u> pink & white varieties of these) & lilies of all kinds, & don't forget the heavenly perennial larkspurs, the divinest azure, rose & saffron tints—sunflowers & hollyhocks, & <u>single</u> dahlias, <u>superb</u> King's flowers, I call them, <u>all colors</u>—& the Oriental poppies, hardy & never failing & gorgeous beyond description. Perennial phloxes, especially the pure white & the rose color. Hydrangea grande flora—all these you know, & the tall Japanese anemones these are heavenly beautiful—dear me—I get out of breath with the perennials before I think of reaching the dear flower seeds for annuals.

She has, in her exhaustive list (and this is not the end of it), produced a dog-eared seed catalogue of her own: a kind of to-do list of a scrupulous gardener or accountant with the most conventional flourishes. "Charming," "desirable," "beautiful," "dear," "divine," "heavenly," "gorgeous"— these words add nothing even as they lengthen out the sentence. To Thaxter's credit, her selection reflects an eye toward an impressionist color palette and her enthusiasm propels the circulation of botanical knowledge, botanical pressings, and seeds among lady correspondents. This American bourgeois continuation of what Theresa Kelley calls "the aesthetic pleasure and invitation to figure that move just beneath the surface of global botanizing as a commercial and imperial venture" retains its ulterior motives. Her interest in the California poppy is both eccentric and conventional by the time of the 1890s, when the poppy had become that embroidery pattern in the *Harper's Bazaar*. Her garden list betrays the decorous quality of extraneous and typical pleasantries, ornamental exclamations, and breathy but well-paced sighs.

Flowers are "dear old friends" that may be marked up on catalogues and bought, economical, profuse, and portable. Pick them by the dozen; throw them out by the dozen. With these things we adorn our lives. On occasion I have felt so, measuring friendship by flowers, sorely used and accessorized.

Letter 5 (undated)

Dear Jules,

Is it our friendship, or a poppy, that invites this correspondence?

In New England, in the nineteenth century, the California poppy's wildness, its sensitivity, its brilliant color made it a kind of spokesperson for the aesthetic. At the end of the century, in California, the flower began to be reclaimed. In poems published in the *Overland Monthly and Out West Magazine* in the 1880s and 1890s, poets—mostly women, now unremembered—turn the poppy into an emblem for Californian history and climate: a miner and a little sun. Made commensurate with the state itself, it conjures up scenes of Californian childhoods. For May Cranmer Duncan, the poppy has a "nameless charm," anonymous, incomparable, and yet common, abundantly flung across the landscape. Affiliated with wealth, with warmth, and with state pride, the California poppy morphs at the end of the century from an eastern ornament—distant and perfect—to a living, western sign.

At the same time, however, even Californians elaborated on the poppy's peculiar aesthetic qualities, particularly its unusually bright color—orange to the point of excess—and its supreme sensitivity. In the Romantic period, poets were obsessed with the "sensitive plant," *Mimosa pudica*, whose leaves curl inwardly when touched. In a British periodical of the 1850s, our poppy is described as so intensely sensitive that it recoils not from a human hand, but from the sky itself: "it closes when a cloud passes." That sensitivity could seem like magic. In 1884, Anna Woodward Truesdall makes the poppy into a play land of "dainty fay-maidens," "elves," a powder pot for "Queen Mab." Traipsing through the plant's bright anatomy, the poem concludes with its characteristic motions: "At dusk thou modestly closest / Thy petals with envious fold."

So the aesthetic of the poppy is both excessive and contingent. *So* common, *so* wild, *so* sensitive, *so* brilliantly colored, and *so* endemic to a particular place that both its belonging and non-belonging draw further attention to it. As a historical agent rather than a document, this sensitive plant, like all plants, has a kind of agency.

Is our friendship similarly both/and, neither here nor there? Is it an ornamental friendship: adjacent and glancing, not quite substantive, nor entirely inhuman? A letter is artifactual and self-referencing, which makes it lively, like the lyric's closed circuit, a voice repeating to itself, and outwardly directed, catching on whatever it passes along the way. Perhaps that direction is not always a clear person, or even a voice.

The truth is, Jules, I have never known how to read or respond to your letters. With other friends, I've walked in circles, up and down hills, in city streets, or at a kitchen table, and our language fell on air and disappeared. With you, there was a postcard once, or several. An old photograph of two girls with the corner torn. And you are right that this is not a letter. We went on walks, bent over stoves, but didn't say what we were thinking. Perhaps none of the earlier ones—the envelope filled with poppy seeds—were appropriately epistolary either. Of what is our friendship composed? Words, words, words. That we stand on opposite banks of some river and see the same glinting things drifting past. A feeling of and, and a feeling of but, of if, of blue, of William James. That we have loved those under similar conditions, and have offered them, once upon a time, to one another. A sentence, an image, a word. Someone else's letter written for someone else. I miss those easy exchanges that inaugurated this era of our education. But not the half empty apartments. Turning to a book as to a friend.

If it's only in written exchanges, or only through the writing of others, that we constellate our affection—but I do not think, finally, that it is *only* that—then we are both typical letter writers and miscreants of the genre. Then we demand to be read but not to be heard.

Letter 6 (Summer)

Dear Gillian,

A few months ago, my copy of Thoreau's *Journal, Volume 1* was recalled to the library, so I began instead with *Volume 2*, or the "Long Book [Fall 1842] - March 1846," with the river trip with his brother and the sighting of a rare hibiscus of which they send news to a friend: "while we shall be floating over the bosom of the Merrimack the flower's friend will be reaching to pluck the blossom on the water of the Concord." The friend is not Thoreau's and his brother's friend, but the flower's friend; we know our friends well enough to know their truer affinities.

I have never been so vain as to imagine any friend to remember me before their own troubles and their own loves; I refuse birthday celebrations because they too strongly tempt disappointment if no one comes and prefer the surer embrace of the one person twined fast to me as the grasses that we wound and braided into bracelets by the edges of the Hetch Hetchy. If Thoreau never married, it was because he had already given himself over to his brother and to his passing. We are, today, at my sister-in-law's wedding. I am like one of those plants that loves the sun, closing and opening its petals to the light. I go to bed early and rise early. The summer makes me tired. Summer is the season of weddings.

How can we deny that our lives are drawn in tighter and tighter orbits like a zoetrope flashing its few images that suffice to create motion, and that is all we need. Our thoughts turn round and round and every time we turn it is to those same loves over and over, the moon, the sea, the pine, the dog, and my love, my love, my love.

I am your friend because you are the flower's friend and not mine. In the glow your eyes cast upon me when I came to your apartment on Alcatraz Ave—you introduced me to fennel in salad—and you had those two paintings, the large black and marigold vase with flowers and the disheveled puppet with Japanese characters scrolling down in columns upside down, that you still have now—that glow was light rubbed off from Whitman or Dickinson. And when you told me that you were reading *Villette* or *Shirley* it was because you were reading what Dickinson had read, absorbing the gold she had imbibed as fresh as seeds placed in water. You never told me why you loved the boy you brought to my apartment seven blocks down from yours, I forget what I made, but you made brussels sprouts with nuts or seeds sprinkled on top, he had steely eyes and had bought you a jar of capers of some extravagant volume that left you wordless. After he died, you told me about dreams of him moving rocks by a river, a methodical displacement, one after the other, that left you chilled cold waking into the night alone.

It was not for me that you spoke of dreams, of poems, or of poppies. You felt instead your own displacement, like river rocks shifting suddenly, the filling in of black water into the absented space. An upstate New York, somewhat Quaker girl-poet who went to Paris, Manhattan, and Japan, and then moved to California. What was she thinking about? He found her writing a poem when he climbed up the wall to her window. Where was he going?

Marriage and a river, two Thoreau boys rafting, provisions of melons and potatoes, and hibiscus woven into the dwarf willows with the grapevines. We are friends because our love is reserved for another, because the words out of our mouths are eaten up by the air, not for our ears, but for our dreams in which we write letters and send messages by way of a farmer in the adjacent meadow to someone who will care more—into our own caring—a self-circular message. Or I am the weaker planet drawn into the ellipse of your thoughts; the adoration of planets and green things growing. Still, we grow. What is a California poppy doing in New England? Growing, growing.

I write this to you from Brattleboro, Vermont, in a little attic room with a stained-glass window of a lotus and cattails on water. It is past midnight, they are playing lawn games in the dark and eating pizza, talking about how the ceremony went. We are surrounded by green hills of trees and shadows, and a sky mottled with silvery clouds— not visible now, but I see it there as I saw it this afternoon, the grass brightening and darkening with movement of the clouds over the sun, and in the distance a red barn in a clearing. Brightness shifting into shadows, shifting into light, into dark, into light, into dark, into night.

P.S. (*unfinished*)

Dear Jules,

Some thoughts on post-scripts:

In New England, California poppies became increasingly rare after the mid-nineteenth century; the peak of their cultivated commonness appears to have been around the 1840s, precisely when Dickinson was assembling her herbarium. The later appropriation of the plant as California's state flower had the effect of repatriating the flower, leaving it to those, our, desiccated hills.

In her series on *Garden Flowers* for "The Pocket Garden Library" published in New York in 1917, Ellen Eddy Shaw notes her interest in documenting the common and the cultivated: "the old-fashioned flowers and popular favorites," which, despite their commonness, are not necessarily "easily identified." I'd like a book like this to tell me the names of all the common garden flowers I walk by in Santa Barbara but still don't know; not to mention, all those trees from the Southern Hemisphere.

"There are books galore," Shaw continues, "to help you to know the wild flowers, but nothing hitherto that has endeavoured to present in a popular manner and in colour the commonest flowers of the cultivated garden." I first began to think about flowers in writing when reading my grandmother's copy of Mrs. William Starr Dana's *How to Know the Wild Flowers*, published in New York at the end of the nineteenth-century, with lyric forays into the "haunts and habits of *our* common wild flowers." No California poppies, there.

In Ellen Eddy Shaw's guide to common garden flowers, there is no California poppy either. There are poppies there, some of which even grow wild in native habitats—England's corn poppy, the Oriental poppy, Iceland poppy, plume poppy, horned poppy, tulip poppy. But "the rare and unusual does not find a place," she writes.

I never saw a California poppy before I moved to California. Nor had I seen all the gardens in New England. Still, their orange was shocking. Far brighter than the tiger lilies we have that line the country roads. Arthur Haines's 2011 guide to non-cultivated native and nonnative plants in New England tells me that Eschscholzia does indeed still grow in Connecticut, Massachusetts, and New Hampshire, in "waste areas, gardens, dumps." Are the poppies that endure sprouting from seeds sewn a century ago? Thoreau and Melville were fascinated with seeds discovered in ancient tombs in Egypt. And after the bombings, poppies emerged around the bodies of fallen soldiers in the ravaged battlefields of World War I. A belated cultivation: how long a seed can stay a seed, and then grow.

In yet another *Guide to the Wildflowers*, from the end of the nineteenth century published in New York (and given to me by another friend), the California poppy does appear: among other wild California flowers. The models for their color plate illustration, complete with a butterfly, "were picked," the author writes, "in Santa Rosa." To "know" the wildflowers, the author advises in her introduction to the volume, "it is necessary that we should seek them in their homes: they seldom come to us."

Are friends the same? Does so much stand between us and them that we need to go looking? A few times in my life, I have been taken unawares by an emergent intimacy. But how often I have gone looking for wildflowers and found nothing wild at all.

I'm trying to decide whether all these framing devices that signal a person is here, writing to another, are in the way, or are the way. Are we making space for the unapproachable in writing to each other?

"My writing apparatus is upon a stand before me, and all things are ready," Dickinson writes to Abiah. But "I have no flowers before me as you had to inspire you."

I was going to say I had gotten the tea tray from upstairs and assembled everything in order to write to you, but it would be a fancy, since I have no tea, no bolstering. Nothing between me and this letter, except the letter that is between me and you. No flowers.

A letter is not a nature walk. Or riding the bus side by side together through the fog. Not like so many things, writing to. Not an analogy for the real thing. Not a lovely weed, misplaced. What is it then? Will these exchanges ever end? Or merely submerge back into the distances between us?

P.P.S.

Dear Jules,

Today, I saw a little side yard of California poppies in New England the morning after we'd talked about geography and the possibility of other lives. Later, I went back to see if they were still there and texted you the evidence.

When I told my mother about our letters, she told me her mother used to plant them—a whole field—at her house in western New York.

Once I had a dream of lying down in that field, feeling the *All*, but there were no poppies in it, or maybe I just didn't know yet what that peripheral color was doing.

LICHEN
WRITING

When did you first get interested in writing, I mean lichen, a writer/ friend asks as we are looking for a beach where we could sit together and read.

The winding roads through Malibu's burned-over district—yellow, purple, black, green. The yellow is gold, the State's imported thirsty grass. We are uncertain of the cause for the lavender-color, lilac-color, or the pronunciation of our supposition—lupine? lupine?—a neat shard for tacking fabric or a stately tree, mined for ship masts in the earlier days of global settlement. I think it is another flower. The black is for the charred trunks of valley oak—deciduous, but these trees won't win back their leaves easily, if ever. The green: parasitic mistletoe, still living and a home for other living things.

I first began thinking about lichen because I was thinking about flowers, I begin. Because, in the mid-1840s, Thomas Wentworth Higginson took a series of walks in search of wildflowers in the vicinity of Cambridge, Massachusetts with a man who would become one of the United States' first devoted lichenologists, Edward Tuckerman. Later, in 1875, Tuckerman updated Edward Hitchcock's original list of plants growing in the vicinity of Amherst—that list which Dickinson, as she wrote to Higginson around the same time, may or may not have read in the winter as a comfort for floral "Absence" in her youth.

The distance between these two lists of plants marks half a century, spanning backward and forward several decades on either side of the Civil War. This continuity of plant-life on either side of that cataclysm stitches the century together, even as human history cleaves it in two. Looking back on his antebellum walks with Tuckerman in a book written at the very end of the century, nostalgically titled *Cheerful Yesterdays*, Higginson recalled the room from which the pair would set out in "all seasons" as "a delightful place to visit,—a large chamber in a rambling old house, with three separate reading-tables, one for botany, one for the study of Coleridge, and one for the Greek drama," and Tuckerman himself as "the simplest-hearted of men, shy, near-sighted, and lovable."

Higginson learned from Tuckerman not only about wildflowers, or Coleridge, but also about the kind of writer he wanted to become: one who could pivot from literature to nature and back again. Into this mix, Higginson later added a trenchant interest in politics and social reform. In the pre-War 1860s, however, no doubt recalling Tuckerman's room with desks for the study of intersecting things, Higginson developed a theory of the co-dependence between literary and naturalist pursuits in his essay called "My Out-Door Study." Higginson's theory was an argument not by but for analogy: "On this flower bank, on this ripple-marked shore, are the true literary models," he wrote. We learn to write by learning to read the material effusions and lines that already compose the natural world.

Tuckerman was drawn to lichen for analogical reasons. In his writings, he admires the object of his study for what he believed it to be: "the lowest forms of vegetable life." That admiration extended from the organism toward what he believed this lowliness modeled: the potential for further human humility. Two decades before Tuckerman began writing about lichen, the Swedenborgian Sampson Reed redefined human "genius" as "the humility which exalts," a recognition that the "growth of the mind" is continuous with all patterns of growth—and decay—in the more-than-human world. Reed and Tuckerman's understanding of the material fallibilities of human intelligence—in a century that did much to contribute to more triumphalist visions of humans, their individual and societal prowess—resonates with recent definitions of the geological era we are living in not as the Anthropocene, but what David Abram calls the Humilicene. If there is no outside to humanness in a planet reshaped by human action from its deepest ocean trenches to the atmospheric edges that separate it from endless space, then that fact should be both a source of humility and humiliation. But Reed already knew that humans were inseparable from the natural world because, like all living things, they retire to rot. And Tuckerman thought that lichen could teach us how to live in closer communion with rock and dirt.

Lichen can seem small, insignificant, occupying one side of a spectrum of visibility that, at the other end, would include things Timothy Morton calls "hyperobjects": stuff too big, or too enduring, to effectively imagine, even with a well-tuned environmental imagination. On the other hand, compared to a microbe, lichen are like charismatic mega-fauna. If the biggest and the smallest stuff among us (an ocean, a cell) lends itself, purely based on scale, to certain degrees of intellectual or imaginative neglect, there are also sliding scales along either end of these spectrums.

Though they don't require a microscope, lichen rarely rise to the fully-fledged visibility of everyday objects. Found endemically in almost every imaginable habitat, they nevertheless merge visibly into other forms. Unless you go to the woods looking for lichen, chances are, you will miss them for the stones, rotting stumps, and living trees on which they grow. And, in any case, even if you have spent some time nose to boulder, breathing in the aroma of foliose forms, there will persist a neglected layer within what can be seen. It's these relations within that sub-visible realm, however, that make lichen compositionally unique.

The lowliness of lichen was apparent to Tuckerman in the 1840s. What wasn't yet visible to him—or to any other viewer at that time—was the chemical make-up of lichen, the string of compounds that appears beside species names in contemporary identification manuals, or the essential symbiosis of what scientists now understand to be a compound organism. Perhaps because of his admiration for lichen as simple, Tuckerman never accepted the symbiotic model of lichen organization, which was introduced several decades after his earliest publication. That theory produced violent debates, prompted by questions, in effect, about whether one thing can be made up of multiple things at once. This debate began when, in 1869 Swiss lichenologist Simon Schwendener described lichen as a living example of a micro-Hegelian master-slave dialectic:

> [T]hese growths are not simple plants, not individuals in the ordinary sense of the word, they are more likely colonies […] Of them, however, one only is in control, whilst the others, forever imprisoned, provide for themselves and their master, nourishment.
>
> This master is a fungus […] a parasite, accustomed to live upon the work of others, its slaves are green Algae, which it […] holds on to and forces into service. It invests them as a spider her prey […] but, whilst the spider sucks out her prey and throws it aside when dead, the Fungus stimulates the Algae […] to more lively activity.

This theory stirred up outrage among some of Schwendener's fellow scientists, who were invested in preserving a vision of the natural world in which species could be neatly filed into separate genres. They were also, like Tuckerman, clearly interested in what lichens might model for human behavior. Writing against Schwendener's analogies of struggle and domination, they came stridently to the defense of the "noble" and "autonomous" lichen.

Schwendener's analogies reflected not only a new biological insight, but also the historical and political world in which these scientists were inescapably entrenched. Each picked the vision of the human world they saw, or wanted to see, and applied it to what remained plastered in gray or rust-red to a rock. More recently, other analogies for what lichen might model have been forwarded: a material "under-commons," by way of Fred Moten and Stefano Harney; in Brenda Hillman's lichen-inspired hybrid journal-poems; or an example of interconnection among individuals for mycologist Merlin Sheldrake. Lichen might be unacknowledged legislators, or webpages riddled with hyperlinks.

What interests me most about all these analogies, though, is not only what they reveal about lichen, or the hopes and disasters of the human worlds that produce and are reflected by such analogies, but what they demonstrate about the fungibility of analogy itself, particularly when applied to any feature of the natural world. Schwendener, in order to describe the mutualism of lichen, is so drawn to analogy that he piles one on top of another. Centuries later, the analogies continue to accumulate. In each instance, analogy rides on top of the literal, pointing to its direct object; that pointing can take place through a series of variations, and still indicate the same, literal, thing. A master and slave. A spider and a fly. A network of mutual aid. A friend and a friend. There is a problem with the form of argument, obviously, when a master might be elided with a friend.

"Is analogy argument?" one of Herman Melville's not-quite-real-ized-human-persons asks. Personification has been another persistent fallacy, wherein we mistake the fullness of a feeling for the fullness of a human life, or recast an inhuman world in human form. What is it within the persistent we have yet to learn? Is repetition a feature of persistence, or the manifestation of an imaginative glitch? When I learned to write an argument, it went like this: they said, I said. He said, she said. I tried writing it into poems, to change the context: we walked to the top of the hill to be closer to the sky. You have a fundamental acceptance of finitude, he said. A green bird in a green tree. A splash of living color on the skin of geologic time. You should know, you said, your words are a small part of the "under-song."

If a human is "an analogist, and studies relations in all objects," as another essayist whose poetry was in his prose once wrote, I still want to know what stands on the other side of the analogy that lichen writing is. If lichen finds its way into writing, which like everything else it does, or if writing is lichen-like, what is the other thing, outside of writing, still in relation, that stays, singing across the dash? Lichen writing, so in—

* * *

In one of his books on lichen, Tuckerman reflects on the importance of using not only "Analogy" but also "Affinity" in the study of plants. Analogy, he defines as two things "which occupy parallel places in different series," and yet "mutually correspond to each other." As in, how a right whale when reduced to bones appears to have a hand. Affinity, on the other hand, he defines as things "which follow in the same series" and because of their proximity "seem mutually to pass into each other." As in, a mother and a child, or a flower and a friend.

Higginson and Tuckerman were not alone within the nineteenth century in their participation in homo-social floral bonding. Within that context, a shared enthusiasm for flowers could harbor, and even provide a language for, indirect forms of intimacy that, for one reason or another, required that indirection. Similarly, a shared passion for the literary has defined, shaped, complicated, vexed, and created space for many of my most meaningful relationships, especially with women. One important friendship, for example, began with a soon-to-be-friend literally reading *A Brave New World* over my shoulder, sometime in the final decade of the twentieth century.

Meanwhile, the longer I am a mother, the more I find that the affinities of pregnancy and early parenthood are revised, written again. Something symbiotic falls apart to be remade in other materials, over and over. This morning, a child told me there are some kinds of long-armed octopi that turn into rocks before turning into plants before turning into animals that live forever. The literal gets caught in the orbit of the literary, drawing basic availability into realms of the impossible. Like a lichen, I said. No, he said, not.

Despite these differences, analogy and affinity are also part of the same series, merging toward if not into each other, in that they are one of many, many, different methods for considering the realms of possible connection between this and this. Just as there are spectrums of visibility, let's say there is also a spectrum of different modes of accounting for these ways one thing resembles, or bonds with, another. Analogy would be at the neglected, bed-rocky bottom, and allegory the airy peak, with simile, metaphor, metonymy ghosting about the Purgatorial middle, and tropes of affiliation—personification, anthropomorphism, etc.—parading disorderly about as the atmosphere grows thin. Affinity is something else, though, as I understand it. Love drawn out from the allegorical charade by the form of a chalky blue-green ruffle on a boulder. The action of stooping to consider, of placing a hand upon another living thing, equally noble and low. Affinity, in writing, is like responsiveness to context while reading. Lichen writing through the winter.

Because analogies can shift from object to object, idea to idea, I don't think they're well-equipped as instigators of change. Affinity depends upon more material encounters, just as any walk through a forest changes it. A path creates an edge, and edges re-pattern lives. Of course, scale matters here as well. The places where Higginson and Tuckerman walked together, in search of wildflowers, had already dramatically changed by the end of the nineteenth century, and would be unrecognizable—no flowers there—today. And the fire-scarred sky above the hill above my garden this fall revealed, again, the planet within vicinity.

Reading around Higginson's notebooks documenting his walks in the 1840s, I found a letter acknowledging receipt of these journals by another scientist decades later, around the time when Higginson was cheerfully remembering Tuckerman and his study. "I have got pleasant glimpses through your spectacles of plant-life in Cambridge and vicinity," the recipient of these notebooks wrote. "It seems scarcely possible that some plants you have noted could ever have grown where you found them – Dear me! The march of improvement is not an unmixed pleasure to us all."

When I lived in Massachusetts, I liked to think about a description from Thoreau's journals of 1851, in which he records getting off the train at "Porter's" one morning, at a spot where the commuter rail still runs westward to Concord, and the T is now burrowed below. He observed "the handsome blue flowers of the Succory," or "Chichorium intybus," a flat ragged pale blue flower I had always known as a child as "cornflower," but which I now realize is a different plant. Thoreau's delight at encountering this flower was premised on the recognition "that within the hour [he] had been whirled into a new botanical region." The distances between Cambridge and Concord were vast enough at that time to encompass different vicinities. But there is another kind of proximity I have found in the living histories that green-things carry, that draws me out of locality, into global repetitions of lowliness.

"I feel a not-unusual affinity," Higginson's correspondent continues, "for any man or woman who has ever used an interleaved botany" and "though I have never stopped to analyze the sensation," as I have been analyzing here, "I found it very difficult to dispossess myself" of a book "that had once been a travelling companion of [yours]."

Just as, looking through the annotations in my grandmother's Northeastern *Peterson*, which I have carried from coast to coast to coast to coast, whose faded cover is faded green, I find the poppy family circled along with certain strains of un-belonging oxalis—which my child chewed on by the fistful this winter in California, where it grows, pervasively, only one half of a reproductive dyad, spreading itself through the soil not by seed but via little node-like bulbs, its flowers yellowy sour above tendrils of eager green—next to marginalia denoting "Home!"

ACKNOWLEDGEMENTS

The essays and letters of this book are experiments in reading with others. Throughout, conversations, encounters, and contexts constitute sources as "Alive" as any archive. As much as possible, I have tried to maintain the privacy of living individuals, while making the authors and texts I draw from legible, and traceable, within the space of my writing. Below, I more directly acknowledge my indebtedness to publications, editors, mentors, and friends, clarify some of the more indirect invocations, and credit directly quoted sources.

First, I'm grateful for Nightboat, and especially to Stephen Motika and Lindsey Boldt, for their patience and insight. Thank you to adam bohannon for making the book look beautiful.

Selections from the book previously appeared in *The Critical Flame*, guest edited by *A. Bradstreet, The LARB Quarterly Journal, Entropy,* and *Litmus,* and *Grand Journal.* Work-in-progress was presented at Practice Space, the Poetic Research Bureau, &Now, ASLE, and Bard College. Thank you to Chloe Garcia Roberts, Mia You, Irene Yoon, Janice Lee, Declan Wiffen, Andrea Quaid, Harold Abramowitz, Michelle Detorie, Laura Vena, Agnes Malinowska, Joela Jacobs, and Alex Benson (who also paid for my dinner!). This book never would have found its current form if Diana Lempel hadn't asked me to consider the seasonal research question, "When is color material?" and to revisit my histories with green.

Fellowships from the Harvard University Center for the Environment, The American Antiquarian Society, and the Emily Dickinson International Society allowed me to read deliberately. Thank you to James Engell, Dan Schrag, and especially Elisa New, for her continued support. Though it is a very indirect revision, this book builds on readings and ideas begun in my dissertation at UC-Berkeley, and developed in an article and book chapter on Emily Dickinson. I am grateful to Samuel Otter, Anne-Lise François, and Michelle Kohler for their guidance of this earlier work.

Thank you to Karen Searcy for taking me on a wildflower walk in the Holyoke Range; the many yearly volunteers in the garden at the Emily Dickinson Museum; and archivists at Amherst and Smith Colleges, and Deerfield Academy, for talking with me about the Hitchcocks and Tuckermans, and showing me Orra White's mushroom album and painted herbarium. Thank you to the mist in Deerfield for making the morning I visited especially spooky.

Poetry in America and the Bard College Language & Thinking Program colleagues and students have kept me perennially in the presence of poems, questions of education, and reminded that writing together is my favorite way to write.

"Of Lilies" is for Joanna Picciotto, who kept asking me to consider them.

Thank you, Jules, for reading and writing with me, and sending seeds, or books, in the mail.

Finally, thank you to these dear interlocutors, whose wisdom and/or provocations appear in these essays, or who made time to read and respond to them: Ayon Maharaj (now Swami Medhananda), Janet Min Lee, Luke Stavrand Woolf, Ana Kielson, Liesl Yamaguchi, Sarah Hannan, RJ Leland, Robin Tremblay-McGaw, Samia Rahimtoola, Anna Goldman, and, over and over, Megan Pugh.

Brian: this book is for you. Though how could there be a book for it? It does not fit inside a book.

NOTES & SOURCES

"Of the Eccho in Green"

Sigmund Freud develops the etymology of the uncanny alluded to here. See Virginia Scott Jenkins's *The Lawn: A History of an American Obsession*, Michael Pollan's "Why Mow? The case against lawns," and Timothy Morton's "Wordsworth Digs the Lawn" for more on the development of that particular patch of green and all that it overwrites and ignores.

"Reading Natural History in the Winter"

Wallace Stevens comments on the in-betweens of seasons in a February, 1935 letter to Robert Frost. I am thinking of Eliza Richards's *Gender and the Poetics of Reception in Poe's Circle* when I recommend Lydia Sigourney and Frances Osgood. I.A. Richards describes a "psychoaesthetics"; CA Conrad develops "(soma)tic rituals."

"Of the Vicinity Of"

Robert L. Herbert, Daria D'Arienzo, and Tekla A. Harms provide much of the context for Edward and Orra's relationship, including Harriet Goodhue's copying of Orra White, who sometimes copied from William Withering; see especially D'Arienzo and Herbert's *Orra White Hitchcock: An Amherst Woman of Art and Science* and Herbert's introduction to a facsimile of Orra's mushroom album. Andrea Wulf's *Founding Gardeners* taught me about Jefferson's anxieties regarding Buffon. Elizabeth Kolbert's *The Sixth Extinction*, particularly her research on Lyell, Darwin, and catastrophic extinction, directly informed my thinking about local extinctions as comings and goings of a different scale. I read Charles C. Mann's *1491* and *1493* as pleasure reading on a road-trip through California and they radically changed my sense of "American" place and time. The term "vegetable genius" is M.H. Abrams's. In her introduction to *Urban Tumbleweed*, Harryette Mullen refers to this conversation between Robert Hass and Linda Gregg. In a November 8, 2007 interview with the UC Berkeley News, Hass comments on this conversation and the importance of including Californian, and scientific, names in poems.

"Imagining Mothering"

My film- and "not a play-play"-making friend is Anisa George. *Animal Animal Mammal Mine* was developed and performed in 2013. Marta Figlerowicz is the one with ideas about genre, though I'm pretty sure she was quoting someone else.

"Poppy/Friend"

The longer citations of Chamisso and Eschscholtz's writing can be found in Susan Delano McKelvey's work, listed below.

"Lichen Writing"

I heard David Abram float the term Humilicene in a room where he was also impersonating walruses and discussing the universal music of breath. Christopher Looby writes about nineteenth-century homo-social floral bonding in "Flowers of Manhood"; Dorri Beam elaborates in *Style, Gender, and Fantasy in Nineteenth-Century American Women's Writing*. The block quote from Schwendener is cited in Charles Plitt's "A Short History of Lichenology." Melville considers analogy in *The Confidence-Man*. Emerson haunts the ending of the first part.

Sources of Direct Quotes

Berger, John. "Ape Theater." In *Why Look at Animals?* New York: Penguin, 2009.

Blake, William. "The Ecchoing Green." In *Songs of Innocence and of Experience*. New York: Oxford, 1967.

Carson, Anne. "On Reading." In *Plainwater: Essays and Poetry*. New York: Vintage Books, 1995.

Chamisso, Adelbert von. *A Voyage Around the World with the Romanzov Exploring Expedition in the Years 1815-1818 in the Brig Rurik, Captain Otto von Kotzèbue*. Ed. and Trans. Henry Kratz. Honolulu: University of Hawaii Press, 1986.

"Curiosities of Physical Geography. No. III." In *A Weekly Miscellany of Amusement and Instruction* 2, no. 46. London, November 17, 1852.

D'Arienzo, Daria. "The 'Union of the Beautiful with the Useful': Through the Eyes of Orra White Hitchcock." *The Massachusetts Review* 51, no. 2 (Summer 2010): 294–336.

Davis, Theo. "'Just apply a weight': Thoreau and the Aesthetics of Ornament." *ELH* 77, no. 3 (Fall 2010): 561–587.

Dickinson, Emily. *The Letters of Emily Dickinson*. Ed. Thomas Johnson. Cambridge: Harvard University Press, 1958.

—. *The Poems of Emily Dickinson (Variorum Edition)*. Ed. R.W. Franklin. Cambridge: Harvard University Press, 1998.

Duncan, May Cranmer. "To the Eschscholtzia." *Overland Monthly and Out West Magazine* (1868–1935), no. 127 (July 1893): 50.

Duncan, Robert. "Often I Am Permitted to Return to a Meadow." In *The Opening of the Field*. New York: Grove Press, 1960.

Emmons, Ebenezer. *Reports on the herbaceous plants and on the quadrupeds of Massachusetts*. Cambridge: Folsom, Wels, and Thurston, 1840.

Eliot, T.S. "The Waste Land." In *The Complete Poems and Plays, 1909-1950*. New York: Harcourt, Brace & World, 1934.

"Embroidery Design." *Harper's Bazaar* 27, no. 3 (Jan 20, 1894): 52.

Emerson, Ralph Waldo. *The Early Lectures of Ralph Waldo Emerson*. Ed. Stephen E. Whicher and Robert E. Spiller. Cambridge: Harvard University Press, 1959.

—. *Essays and Lectures*. New York: Library of America, 1983.

Goethe, Johann Wolfgang von. *Theory of Colours*. Trans. Charles Lock Eastlake. London: John Murray, 1840.

Gould, Augustus A. *Report on the Invertebrata of Massachusetts, Comprising the Mollusca, Crustacea, Annelida, and Radiata*. Cambridge: Folsom, Wells, and Thurston Printers, 1841.

Haines, Arthur. *Flora Novae Angliae*. New Haven: Yale University Press, 2011.

Herbert, Robert L. "Introduction." In *Fungi selecti picti* (1821). Watercolors by Orra White Hitchcock. Northampton: Smith College, 2011.

Herbert, Robert L. and Daria D'Arienzo. *Orra White Hitchcock: An Amherst Woman of Art and Science*. Hanover: University Press of New England, 2011.

Higginson, Thomas Wentworth. *Cheerful Yesterdays*. Cambridge: Riverside Press, 1898.

———. "My Out-Door Study" and "Saints and Their Bodies." In *Out-door Papers*. Boston: Ticknor and Fields, 1863.

———. "Preface." In *Poems of Emily Dickinson*. First series. Ed. Mabel Loomis Todd and Thomas Wentworth Higginson. Boston: Roberts Brothers, 1890.

———. "Thomas Wentworth Higginson field notebooks," including letter from L.L. Dame, Archives of the Gray Herbarium, Harvard University, 1841–1894.

Hitchcock, Edward. *Catalogue of Plants Growing Without Cultivation in the Vicinity of Amherst College*. Amherst, 1829.

———. *Religious Lectures on Peculiar Phenomena in the Four Seasons: Delivered to the Students in Amherst College in 1845, 1847, 1848 and 1849*. Amherst: J.S. & C. Adams, 1850.

Holmes, Oliver Wendell. "A Physiology of Versification—Harmonies of Organic & Animal Life." *Boston Medical Surgical Journal* 92 (January 7, 1875): 6–9.

The Holy Bible (Philadelphia, 1843), 1 Corinthians XV: 32, 55, 35–38. Web. Emily Dickinson's Bible. EDR8 Bible. English. 1843. Houghton Library.

Jefferson, Thomas. *Notes on the State of Virginia*, 1785. Widely available.

Keats, John. *The Selected Letters of John Keats*. Ed. Lionel Trilling. New York: Farrar, Straus, and Young, 1951.

Kincaid, Jamaica. "Just Reading." *The New Yorker* 69, no. 6 (March 29, 1993): 51–54.

Knausgaard, Karl Ove. *My Struggle: Book 2*. Trans. Don Bartlett. New York: Farrar, Straus, and Giroux, 2013.

Lounsberry, Alice. *A Guide to the Wildflowers*. New York: F.A. Stokes, 1899.

Lukács, György. "The Foundering of Form Against Life: Søren Kierkegaard and Regine Olsen." In *Soul and Form*. Ed. John T. Sanders & Katie Terezakis. Trans. Anna Bostock. New York: Columbia University Press, 2010.

Lukina, Tatiana Arkadevna. *Johann Friedrich Eschscholtz: 1793–1831*. Trans. Wilma C. Follette. Mill Valley: RAM, 2009.

Mantel, Hilary. "The Rights of Women Under President Trump." *The New Yorker*, November 14, 2016. Web.

McKelvey, Susan Delano. "Eschscholtz and Von Chamisso Spend a Month at the Bay of San Francisco." *Fremontia* 26, 1998.

Melville, Herman. *Pierre, or the Ambiguities*. Evanston: Northwestern University Press, 1971.

———. *The Writings of Herman Melville, Volume Fourteen: Correspondence*. Chicago: Northwestern-Newberry, 1993.

———. *The Confidence-Man: His Masquerade*. Evanston: Northwestern University Press, 2002.

Morton, Timothy. *Hyperobjects: Philosophy and Ecology after the End of the World*. Minneapolis: University of Minnesota Press, 2013.

Nietzsche, Friedrich. *The Gay Science*. Ed. Bernard Williams. Trans. Josefine Nauckhoff. New York: Cambridge University Press, 2001.

Phelps, Almira Lincoln. *Familiar Lectures on Botany* (1829). New York: F.J. Huntington, 1853.

Ramazani, Jahan. "The Local Poem in a Global Age." *Critical Inquiry* 43, No. 3 (Spring 2017): 670–696.

Ransom, John Crowe. *The New Criticism*. Norfolk: New Directions, 1941.

Reed, Sampson. "Oration on Genius" (1821) and "Observations on

the Growth of the Mind" (1826). In *Transcendentalism: A Reader*.
Ed. Joel Myerson. New York: Oxford University Press, 2000.

Schwendener, Simon. Qtd. in Charles C. Plitt, "A Short History
of Lichenology." *The Bryologist* 22, no. 6 (November, 1919):
77–85.

Shaw, Ellen Eddy. *Garden Flowers of Summer, Vol 2.* New York:
Doubleday, 1917.

Shelley, Mary. "Introduction." In *Frankenstein*. London: Henry
Colburn and Richard Bentley, 1831.

Shelley, Percy Bysshe. "A Defence of Poetry." In *Essays, Letters from
Abroad, Translations and Fragments*. London: Edward Moxon,
1840.

Gertrude, Stein. "Before the Flowers of Friendship faded Friendship
faded. Written on a poem by George Hugnet." Paris: Plain
Edition, 1931.

Teschemacher, J.E. "Flowers in Blossom in October." *Horticultural
Register and Gardener's Magazine*. Vol. I. Boston: George C.
Barrett, 1835: 454–456.

Thaxter, Celia. *An Island Garden*. Boston: Houghton Mifflin, 1894.
———. *Letters of Celia Thaxter*. Boston: Houghton Mifflin, 1895.

Thoreau, Henry David. *Faith in a Seed: The Dispersion of Seeds and
Other Late Natural History Writings*. Ed. Bradley P. Dean. Covelo,
CA: Island Press, 1993.

———. "Natural History in Massachusetts." In *The Dial* (July 1842).
———. *The Writings of Henry D. Thoreau: Journals 1–8*. Princeton:
Princeton University Press, 1982-2002.

Truesdell, Amelia Woodward. "The California Eschscholtzia."
Overland Monthly and Out West Magazine (1868-1935), no. 5 (May
1884): 520.

Tuckerman, Edward. *An Enumeration of North American Lichens.* Cambridge: John Owen, 1845.

Whitman, Walt. "Song of Myself." In *Leaves of Grass.* New York, 1855.

Wood, Alphonso. *A Class-Book of Botany: The Elements of Botanical Science* and *The Natural Orders, Illustrated by a Flora of the Northern, Middle, and Western States, particularly of the United States north of the capitol, lat. 33¾.* Boston: Crocker & Brewster, 1853.

Zolotow, Charlotte. *Over and Over.* New York: Harper Collins, 1957.

GILLIAN OSBORNE is a writer and educator, raised in upstate New York and currently living in California. The co-editor of *Ecopoetics: Essays in the Field*, she teaches and designs curriculum for Poetry in America and the Bard College Institute for Writing & Thinking. Her poetry, essays, and criticism have appeared in publications such as the *Boston Review, Los Angeles Review of Books Quarterly Journal, The New Republic, Interdisciplinary Studies in Literature & the Environment,* and *The New Emily Dickinson Studies.*

NIGHTBOAT BOOKS

Nightboat Books, a nonprofit organization, seeks to develop audiences for writers whose work resists convention and transcends boundaries. We publish books rich with poignancy, intelligence, and risk. Please visit nightboat.org to learn about our titles and how you can support our future publications.

The following individuals have supported the publication of this book. We thank them for their generosity and commitment to the mission of Nightboat Books:

Kazim Ali
Anonymous (5)
Jean C. Ballantyne
The Robert C. Brooks Revocable Trust
Amanda Greenberger
Rachel Lithgow
Anne Marie Macari
Elizabeth Madans
Elizabeth Motika
Thomas Shardlow
Benjamin Taylor
Jerrie Whitfield & Richard Motika

In addition, this book has been made possible, in part, by grants from the National Endowment for the Arts, the New York City Department of Cultural Affairs in partnership with the City Council, the New York State Council on the Arts Literature Program, and the Topanga Fund.